" 'What do you own?' she asked.
'For surely everything belongs to God.
We may only have the use of things,
temporarily, while in the world.
What is important
is not how much or how little we have.
For material opulences
such as wealth, beauty, name, and fame,
are in themselves neither good nor bad.
A knife in the hands of a surgeon may save your life.
A knife in the hands of a murderer
may take your life.
So it is not things which are good or bad,
but the use made of them.
And the perfection of life,
is not to give up everything,
but to use everything,
in the service of good.
In the service of God.”

Mother Rytasha

The Angel of Bengal

by Razzaque Khan

A Young Couple's Blueprint for Managing Money

Building Relationships Through Faith and Financial Planning

Bonnie Baron Scully
Certified Financial Planner

Acknowledgements

There are so many people to thank for their contributions to this book and to my life. Barbara Osborn, my sister, was the initial inspiration to me as together we conceived the idea of a comprehensive organized file to manage finances. She and my mother, Patricia Baron, have been a continuing source of encouragement.

My heartfelt gratitude is extended to Kelly Davis for her expert editing and feedback and to all those who assisted with proofreading, including Bart Boyer, Dick Wood, Reese Lasher, Erin and Dan White, and Ray Fonseca.

I wish to thank Forrest Greene not only for his excellent graphic design but also for his creative ability to transform a manuscript into a book.

I would like to especially thank Brenda Sconyers, who coordinated this project from an idea to finished product. She always connected me with the people I needed, kept me on track, and shared my vision.

The artistic contributions of John Warner, Dana Irwin, and Ami Tomlo Dickinson are greatly appreciated.

Thanks to Craig Williamson, Bill Westcott, Mary Trigg Scully and Barbara Hemphill for their technical advice.

I thank my children, Amanda and Johnny, for their patience and love, and for motivating me to complete this work.

My heartfelt appreciation to my husband, Bob, for the life we share that inspired this book, for all of his loving feedback, his confidence in me, and his belief in this project.

I thank Sister Marie Bruchette, Fr. Frank Cancro, Fr. Vince Alagia, Father Morris Boyd, Gerald Carter, and Ken Mesker for their encouragement and support. I thank all those couples I have counseled for letting me make a contribution to their lives, and I thank God for His many gifts, and for giving me the opportunity to share those gifts with others.

Scully, Bonnie Baron.
    The Scully Files: A Young Couple's Blueprint for
Managing Money: Building Relationships Through
Faith and Financial Planning / Bonnie Baron Scully.
— 1st Edition
p. cm.
LCCN:00-190810
ISBN: 0-9670260-9-1

1. Couples—Finance, Personal. 2. Married people—
Finance, Personal. I. Title.

HG179.S38 2000   332.024'065
                                        QBI00-500

Dedicated to Bob
my soul mate on the journey
and to my children Amanda and Johnny
the joy of my life

This workbook evolved from three distinct sources:

First, in my counseling of couples preparing for marriage, I wanted to provide a reference they could use after our sessions. I wanted them to have a summary of our conversation on comprehensive financial planning and the forms they would need to organize their finances as they began their lives together. My first book, *The Scully Files - Organizing Your Finances* was in answer to that need. The response to it was so positive that I decided to expand it into *The Scully Files: A Young Couple's Blueprint for Managing Money*.

Secondly, as my husband pursued his gift of caring for patients and their health needs, I evolved as the manager of our finances. I wanted to have all of our important papers in one place so they were easily accessed and I didn't waste precious time together digging through files.

Lastly, as I worked with my parents on their finances over the years, especially as my father faced his final years, he desired so much to have all his financial affairs in order for my mother and all of his children. Well, here it is, Dad, and this is my thank-you for all your love and inspiration.

A Young Couple's Blueprint for Managing Money

Building Relationships Through Faith and Financial Planning

CONTENTS

The Philosophy of Money

"Lord, you have given me so much. Grant me one thing more:
a grateful heart. Amen."
—My Grandmother's favorite prayer.

Bonnie Baron Scully

A priest once told me that most problems in marriage concern either sex or money, and most of the problems concerning sex stem from problems concerning money. With half of all marriages ending in divorce and most couples citing financial problems as the major contributing factor to the breakup of their marriage, a strong financial philosophy and foundation is imperative to the beginning of a successful marriage.

The emphasis on money in our society has intensified to the point that, when we discuss money, it evokes feelings of anxiety and insecurity, rather than possibility. Perhaps that is why we dread talking about, and avoid handling, our finances.

The purpose of this book is to stimulate a positive concept of money based on spiritual values, to enable you to communicate openly and effectively, and to help you create a plan for handling your finances that will bring you peace and assist you in reaching financial independence.

As we approach the subject of money, if we are not grounded in faith, we seek money as an object to be acquired and kept. We are instead grounded in fear—fear of limited supply. Because we can only depend on ourselves, we feel the need to hoard money, and are not open to the divine flow of God's gifts, which leads to real prosperity.

When we are grounded in faith, we no longer have to shoulder the responsibility of being the source of our wealth. We turn that over to God and His unconditional love, trusting in His Will and believing in His unlimited supply to provide for us all that we need.

We have all been blessed with many unique God-given gifts: our talents, our intelligence, our faith, our country, our families, and our friends. As we develop our individual talents and use these gifts to serve others, our talents then have value which generates money—money that is meant to be appreciated by putting it to good use!

Remember that God is the source of all gifts—we are the stewards. The good steward does not put money in the ground, but uses it in positive ways to provide for his needs and goals (spending and saving), to generate more money (through investing), and to help others (gifting). These positive uses of money each allow the "gift-flow" to pass on and multiply.

Instead of worrying about the future, we can begin each day with a prayer of thanksgiving for what we have been given, and see how we can best use the gifts of our talents and treasure to generate wealth to help our families and our world.

When we are in love, we especially avoid discussing money. We soon realize that we come from different economic backgrounds, and to avoid conflict, we don't bring up our concerns.

Some of us have come from poor families and have learned to fear (or expect) a lack of money, even if we become rich. Some of us have come from wealthy families and have never had to learn to manage money, or have rejected the opulence we have seen misused. Some of us have come from modest families with financial security, but we have parents who experienced the Great Depression, and shared some pretty frightening stories with us.

We need to be open to and sensitive to our differences, learn from one another, find common ground in order to resolve our conflicts, and see this process as an opportunity to share ourselves intimately with one another.

One adage is true—"money does not buy happiness." I have known some people with very little to their name who are fearful and sad, while others with little money have a wonderful sense of freedom and a greater understanding of the gifts that really make us rich.

I have known very wealthy people who are terribly unhappy and others that are thoroughly enjoying the fruits of their labor and what that enables them to do. Generating money is good when we use it wisely.

No matter how much or how little money you have right now, it is just the right amount. There will always be people who have more than you do, and there will always be people who have less than you do. Your happiness comes from what you do with what you have right now.

As you read through the various sections of this book, it is important to be aware of our different backgrounds and attitudes about money, keep a sense of humor, be patient, and come from love as you communicate about money. And communicate you must!

When my father passed away, he left us so much more than an inheritance; he left us a legacy. He always taught me that when you die, you take nothing with you, but you do leave something behind. You leave that part of you that you shared with others, the example of the life that you led, the good that you did for your fellow man, and how you served your God.

If any of us were to die today, we would not miss the job or the money. We would miss the time with our families and dear friends, the joy and richness of the simple pleasures of life, and the chance we had to make a positive difference in this world.

When we think of money as a gift that God has entrusted to us as His stewards, we experience an immeasurable sense of freedom that allows us to get on with living, loving, and just being an instrument of God's plan.

I hope this book empowers you to enjoy the adventure of planning your financial future together and to treasure the gift of love you have been given.

How to Use This Book
Each section in this workbook covers a specific area of financial planning.

Financial planning binder

As you work through the book, you can create your own financial planning notebook that will pull together all of your critical information and serve as an invaluable reference. After reading the narrative summary of each chapter, make copies of the forms for that section (located at the back of the book). Complete these forms in pencil, three-hole punch them, and put them in your own binder. You can add labeled divider tabs to easily access each section. You can use your notebook at tax time, to review your finances monthly, and to have all your important financial information easily accessible.

File Cabinet

Keep a file with the following folders at your desk:

> Bills to pay
>
> Paid receipts
>
> Bank statements
>
> Brokerage statements
>
> Brokerage transactions
>
> Tax information, including:
>
>> Business receipts
>>
>> Charitable contributions
>>
>> W-2s
>>
>> End-of-year statements

As important financial papers arrive during the month, follow this procedure:

Bills: Put in "bills to pay" file and, once a week, pay whatever is due.

Receipts: Put any paid tax-related receipts you need to save in the "tax information" file. Put major purchase/warranty receipts in "paid receipts" file.

Bank statements: Balance your statements and record information on the Monthly Income/Expense form in your binder. Then file under "bank statements."

Brokerage statements: From your December 31st statement, record your beginning holdings on the Portfolio Summary form and put in your binder. File monthly brokerage statements in the "brokerage statements" file.

Brokerage trades: Enter transaction information on the transactions page in the investment section of your binder, and place the confirmation in the "brokerage transactions" file.

Tax information: Charitable contributions should be recorded in the appropriate section of your binder. Put letters of acknowledgement and receipts of contributions in the "tax information" file. Any other tax-related information and receipts should be put in the "tax information" file as well.

After your taxes have been filed, you can file a copy of your tax return, the contents of the tax information file, and your monthly bank and brokerage statements for the year in a manila envelope with the year marked on the front. Now you are ready to start another organized year!

This workbook is designed to:

Simplify Your Life—
By providing a system that keeps your current financial situation at your fingertips.

Save You Time—
Time that could be spent pursuing those things in your life that are most meaningful to you.

Organize Your Paperwork—
All the important documents and statements which come across your desk each month.

Enhance Your Relationship—
by improving communication about money.

Bring You Peace of Mind—
concerning your financial future.

Get Your *Financial* House In Order

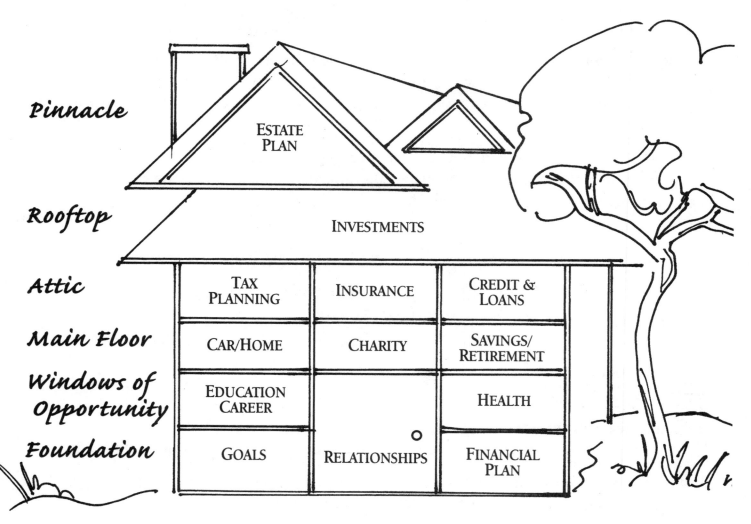

Pinnacle — ESTATE PLAN

Rooftop — INVESTMENTS

Attic — TAX PLANNING | INSURANCE | CREDIT & LOANS

Main Floor — CAR/HOME | CHARITY | SAVINGS/RETIREMENT

Windows of Opportunity — EDUCATION CAREER | | HEALTH

Foundation — GOALS | RELATIONSHIPS | FINANCIAL PLAN

Comprehensive financial planning involves the coordination of many areas of your life. Like building a home, you need a strong foundation—and the building blocks need to be built on each other, cemented with love. Each chapter in this book is meant to help you build your financial plan. So, let us begin to get your financial house in order.

Sharing Ourselves
The Heart of the Matter

Photograph © S&S Photography

Before we begin to take a comprehensive look at all the areas of financial planning and how they can work together to build a secure financial future, let's look at what is really important in the big picture—LOVE.

God is Love, and as the CFO, the Chief Financial Officer in our lives, and the third partner in this marriage relationship, we first turn to Him for direction and to recognize the gifts He has given us to handle this area of our lives and our relationships.

Take some time to reflect on and write your responses to the statements on the following pages. There's one page for each of you to fill out. This will help you to begin to communicate more intimately about your relationship with money.

Sharing Ourselves

Her Responses

This is what I heard about money when I was growing up... _____

_____

_____

_____

_____

It made me feel... _____

_____

_____

_____

_____

My greatest fear concerning money is... _____

_____

_____

_____

My greatest hope for our financial future is... _____

_____

_____

_____

My greatest strength when it comes to handling finances is... _____

_____

_____

_____

My greatest weakness in money management is... _____

_____

_____

_____

The one thing I most want to share with you concerning our money is... _____

_____

_____

_____

His Responses

This is what I heard about money when I was growing up... _____

_____

_____

_____

_____

It made me feel... _____

_____

_____

_____

_____

My greatest fear concerning money is... _____

_____

_____

_____

My greatest hope for our financial future is... _____

_____

_____

_____

My greatest strength when it comes to handling finances is... _____

_____

_____

_____

My greatest weakness in money management is... _____

_____

_____

_____

The one thing I most want to share with you concerning our money is... _____

_____

_____

_____

GOAL SETTING
What Are Your Dreams?

One of my favorite days of the year is the day my husband and I set aside to plan our goals. Our day begins with a prayer of thanksgiving for all the blessings of the past year, including all the joys and successes, as well as all the challenges that have helped us grow closer to God and to each other. Then we take time to celebrate the moment—where we are right now—and how good it is just the way it is, even with all the unfinished business and concerns.

After a look to the past and the present, we have the pleasure of sharing all the dreams we have for the future. It renews the hopes and dreams of our wedding day as we began our life together. That is why I recommend that you designate a special night at least once a year (around the time of your anniversary, in January as you begin a new year, or in April after you file your taxes) to review your goals and to plan for your future.

If you are engaged or married, create an atmosphere conducive to envisioning the dreams you wish to create together in the year ahead, the next five years, and into retirement. It is so important to write down the things that you want to accomplish or attain in your life because, as has repeatedly been shown, writing them down on paper helps to make them actually happen. I once found a list of five-year goals I had written down and almost all of them had been accomplished within three years, even though I had lost the list. Subconsciously I was moving toward my dreams.

Take some time to individually reflect on and visualize your life. Write down your dreams on the individual goals worksheets. You don't need to fill in every blank; rather, fill in what comes to mind initially and complete these forms as new ideas present themselves. Then share and talk about your goals with one another.

After you share your dreams, you can write down the goals you have in common on the "our goals worksheet." This list will enable you to prioritize how you wish to spend your time and money as a couple.

Finally, list any other individual goals that you want to accomplish in the near future so you can support each other. One of the most beautiful aspects of married life is helping each other to reach your potential and use your gifts to make a difference in the world. Even your wildest dreams can be accomplished when you say, "You can do it, honey. We can do it. Let's go for it!"

One of the greatest benefits of goal setting is preparing for a family. Too often couples get married while both are working, and they buy a home and many other possessions on credit. They are so much in debt by the time they decide to start a family that they both **have** to work to pay the bills. If you plan for the future, it is possible to have the choice for one of you to stay home after your children are born.

After you finish your goal-setting exercise, notice how many of your goals have to do with money and how many actually have more to do with time and people. Identifying which goals require money will help you allocate your funds in both the long and short term, but often our most meaningful goals have more to do with free time and our relationships.

Her Goals

Date_____

	1 Year	5 Years	Retirement
1. SPIRITUAL			
2. FAMILY			
3. HEALTH			
4. PROFESSIONAL			
5. COMMUNITY			
6. FINANCIAL			
7. MAJOR PURCHASES			
8. VACATIONS			
9. SOCIAL			
10. HOBBIES & AVOCATIONS			
11. DREAMS			
12. OTHER			

For your personal use, a copy of this form can be found in the back of this book.

Goal Setting

His Goals

Date_____

	1 Year	5 Years	Retirement
1. SPIRITUAL			
2. FAMILY			
3. HEALTH			
4. PROFESSIONAL			
5. COMMUNITY			
6. FINANCIAL			
7. MAJOR PURCHASES			
8. VACATIONS			
9. SOCIAL			
10. HOBBIES & AVOCATIONS			
11. DREAMS			
12. OTHER			

For your personal use, a copy of this form can be found in the back of this book.

Our Goals

Date_____

	1 Year	5 Years	Retirement
1. SPIRITUAL			
2. FAMILY			
3. HEALTH			
4. PROFESSIONAL			
5. COMMUNITY			
6. FINANCIAL			
7. MAJOR PURCHASES			
8. VACATIONS			
9. SOCIAL			
10. HOBBIES & AVOCATIONS			
11. DREAMS			
12. OTHER			

For your personal use, a copy of this form can be found in the back of this book.

NET WORTH STATEMENT
What You Have

The net worth statement is a snapshot of your financial situation at a given moment. It is a list of all you own and all you owe. The difference between these two is your net worth. (All we own minus all we owe = our net worth.)

Assets include current assets, long-term investment assets, and personal use assets.

Current assets are assets that are fairly easily converted into cash, including cash and brokerage accounts.

Long-term investment assets include retirement accounts and any other investments held for long-term appreciation.

Personal use assets include your personal possessions and real estate.

Liabilities include anything that you owe, including mortgages, credit card debt, and any loans you might have.

To complete the Annual Net Worth Statement in this section, make a list of the value of all your assets and total it. Then list and total all liabilities. Subtract your total liabilities from your total assets to determine your current net worth.

For couples who are engaged, it is helpful to first assess your individual net worth and then combine all assets and liabilities on one sheet in a common net worth statement.

Once a year, at least, you will want to update your Annual Net Worth Statement with the goal of increasing your net worth. It gives you a tremendous sense of accomplishment to see your financial worth grow, and an increasing net worth is the clearest reflection of your financial growth.

The Net Worth History form, which is included, provides the opportunity for you to watch your net worth grow from year to year. On this form, you simply list your total assets, total liabilities, and net worth. By comparing year to year, you begin to realize how appreciating assets will help you grow financially.

If your net worth is increasing, be sure to take the time to appreciate what, through the grace of God, you have been able to accomplish. If your net worth has not increased, try to determine why not, but keep it in perspective. Not every year will be a winner, but if the trend is upward you are moving in the right direction. What can you learn from this? Where is God leading you?

Annual Net Worth Statement   *Date*_____

ASSETS
Current Assets

CASH/CHECKING . . . .   _____

CASH/CHECKING 2 . . . . . .   _____

SAVINGS . . . .   _____

STOCKS . . . .   _____

BONDS . . . .   _____

MUTUAL FUNDS . . . .   _____

OTHER . . . .   _____

OTHER . . . .   _____

OTHER . . . .   _____

TOTAL CURRENT ASSETS
Long-Term Investment Assets

IRA . . . .   _____

IRA . . . .   _____

OTHER RETIREMENT . . . . .   _____

OTHER . . . .   _____

OTHER . . . .   _____

Personal Use Assets

AUTOMOBILES . . . .   _____

PERSONAL PROPERTY . . . .   _____

HOME . . . .   _____

REAL ESTATE . . . .   _____

OTHER . . . .   _____

OTHER . . . .   _____

OTHER . . . .   _____

TOTAL LONG-TERM ASSETS . . . . . ._____

TOTAL ASSETS . . . .   _____

LIABILITIES

CREDIT CARD BALANCE . . .   _____

_____

_____

Loans:	*Balance*	*Interest Rate*	*Annual Payment*
HOME	_____	_____	_____
AUTOMOBILES	_____	_____	_____
OTHER	_____	_____	_____
OTHER	_____	_____	_____

TOTAL LIABILITIES . . . .   _____

NET WORTH . . . .   _____

TOTAL LIABILITIES AND NET WORTH . . . .   _____

For your personal use, a copy of this form can be found in the back of this book.

Net Worth History

YEAR	TOTAL ASSETS	−	TOTAL LIABILITIES	=	NET WORTH
2000	_____		_____		_____
2001	_____		_____		_____
2002	_____		_____		_____
2003	_____		_____		_____
2004	_____		_____		_____
2005	_____		_____		_____
2006	_____		_____		_____
2007	_____		_____		_____
2008	_____		_____		_____
2009	_____		_____		_____
2010	_____		_____		_____
2011	_____		_____		_____
2012	_____		_____		_____

Net Worth

Monthly Account Balances

Accounts	JAN	FEB	MAR	APR	MAY	JUN	JUL	AUG	SEP	OCT	NOV	DEC

For your personal use, a copy of this form can be found in the back of this book.

INCOME/EXPENSE STATEMENT
What You Earn and Spend

At the end of the month, do you wonder what happened to all that money you had? Nobody likes the idea of having a budget. It makes you feel that you have to limit yourself.

In reality, an income/expense statement is just a plan for how you choose to give your money away. It puts you in control of distributing the money you have created through the use of your talents.

One of the greatest mistakes I have seen people make is that if they make $20,000, they spend $20,000, and if they make $200,000, they spend $200,000. Since they have not allocated any of their earnings for taxes, savings, and emergencies, at the end of the year they will be in debt. With increasing tax brackets, the more money they earn, the more in debt they will be!

If you allocate for taxes (15-30%), savings and retirement funding (10-20% invested properly), and charitable giving (10%), and keep your living expenses to 50-60% of your gross pay, you will be rich. If you spend everything you make, you will get further and further into debt.

This habit of spending 50-60% of what you earn, if started early, will prevent a dependence on credit, eliminate tremendous stress, and set you on the path to financial security.

If this seems impossible to you, make one of your goals and prayers to find the joy in life that comes from making your lifestyle fit your budget. It is a lot more fun to do inexpensive things with no stress than expensive things on credit!

Take on the challenge that society and the media present to us concerning what we need. There is so little that we really need and so much that we are being convinced we want, even when it puts us into distressing debt. I treasure the memories of starting out small: living in student housing, taking walks, pot luck dinners with friends, buying pizza with leftover change, and saving up for a date night once a month. I also remember times I spent way too much on clothes I grew tired of and food that was wasted.

Take a stand now to be in control and choose carefully who will get the money you have. If you don't want to give it away to the utility company, turn the lights out! If you don't want to throw it away as interest payments, don't buy on credit. If you want the freedom of opportunity, don't put all your money into big house or car payments. Build a strong foundation and enjoy the lifestyle you can afford right now, however humble.

Material possessions are more greatly appreciated and enjoyed when you delay the gratification until they are easily affordable and you have saved for them because they were that important to you. When in doubt about a purchase, sleep on it. Then decide if you really need or want it or if you are just being influenced by the world's standards.

To complete the ANNUAL INCOME/EXPENSES page:

Last year: Column 1

As you prepare to do your taxes, you will have much of the information you need to record your income and expenses over the past year in column 1, and to observe your spending habits.

Coming year: Column 2

In the second column, estimate what you plan to spend in each category for the year ahead. Be generous with yourself in the areas that are most important to you, and try to cut back in areas where you think you are giving away more than you want to. I always encourage couples to allocate a certain amount of individual spending money each month for your personal enjoyment. No one wants to feel that all money is budgeted and there is nothing just for fun.

Monthly allocation: Column 3

To determine your monthly allocation, divide each amount in column 2 by 12 to determine how much you plan to spend monthly in each category during the coming year.

Monthly Income/Expense Sheet:

Some people like to keep track of their expenses daily or weekly. At least once a month, when your bank statement arrives, you should figure how your plan compares to what you really spent. The Monthly Income/Expense Sheet provides this opportunity for you to observe, compare, and adjust your spending habits from month to month.

When we were first married (with very limited income), it made a tremendous difference to keep track of where money was spent. The time you spend each month will instill in you an awareness of expenditures and control of your finances, rather than a feeling of money slipping through your fingers. If you have concrete records of how you spent your money, you won't wonder what happened to it at the end of the month.

If you are proficient on computers, there are several computer software programs that you can utilize to pay bills and categorize expenses, balance your bank statements, and print out an income/expense statement. I strongly recommend that you use a computer program if possible. It will simplify your record keeping and save you time and money in the long run. Quicken and Microsoft Money are two of the most popular programs you may want to look into. If you do use a computer program, just print out your monthly income/expense statements, three-hole punch them, and put them in your binder for quick reference.

At the end of the month, if you find you are spending more than you are bringing in, you have three choices: you can either reduce spending, increase income, or both.

How can you increase your income? Where can you reduce expenses? To generate more money, use your imagination! Money comes from ideas—and big money comes from big ideas. Think creatively. Where are you needed? How can you best use your talents to serve others?

Annual Income/Expenses

	Last Year	This Year's Plan	Monthly Divide Column 2 By 12
INCOME			
SALARY (Husband)			
SALARY (Wife)			
OTHER			
OTHER			
OTHER			
TOTAL INCOME			
OUTGO			
GOD (CHARITY)			
CAESAR (TAXES)			
MY DREAMS (SAVINGS)			
MY FUTURE (RETIREMENT) . .			
NET INCOME			
LIVING EXPENSES			
HOUSING			
HOUSEHOLD/REPAIRS			
FOOD			
CLOTHING			
HEALTH			
EDUCATION			
UTILITIES			
INSURANCE			
TRANSPORTATION			
LOANS			
ENTERTAINMENT/GIFTS			
ACTIVITIES			
CASH/MISCELLANEOUS			
OTHER			
OTHER			
OTHER			
OTHER			
TOTAL OUTGO			
NET			

For your personal use, a copy of this form can be found in the back of this book.

Monthly Income/Expenses

Year _____

	JAN	FEB	MAR	APR	MAY	JUNE	JULY	AUG	SEPT	OCT	NOV	DEC
INCOME												
SALARY (H)												
SALARY (W)												
OTHER												
OTHER												
OTHER												
TOTAL INCOME												
OUTGO												
GOD (CHARITY)												
CAESAR (TAXES)												
MY DREAMS (SAVINGS)												
MY FUTURE (RETIREMENT)												
NET INCOME												
LIVING EXPENSES												
HOUSING												
HOUSEHOLD/REPAIRS												
FOOD												
CLOTHING												
HEALTH												
EDUCATION												
UTILITIES												
INSURANCE												
TRANSPORTATION												
LOANS												
ENTERTAINMENT/GIFTS												
ACTIVITIES												
CASH/MISCELLANEOUS												
OTHER												
OTHER												
OTHER												
OTHER												
TOTAL OUTGO												
NET												

CHARITABLE GIVING
It Will Come Back to You

Contributing to our church and our favorite charities gives us the opportunity to really make a difference in our community, our nation, and our world.

Make it a goal and a habit to give back 10% of what you are given. You can be assured that 10% of the profit from the sale of this book will be contributed to charity. I know from experience that you will see far more than what you give returned to you in ways you may not expect.

Don't wait until you have "more money" before you give, or you will miss the joy of giving. The personal satisfaction of helping others, of sharing your gifts with others no matter how little or how much you have, gives you an immense sense of accomplishment, personal satisfaction, and peace.

When you are first starting out, if money is just too tight, consider giving of your time and talents. Your community and church can benefit from that treasure as well as from money.

Here are some of the other benefits of charitable giving

1. If you itemize, you can reduce your taxable income by deducting contributions to a recognized charity, including mileage expenses for volunteer work.

2. You can donate your appreciated stock and not have to be taxed on the capital gain. For example, you buy a stock for $1,000 and donate it when it is worth $3,000. The charity gets $3,000 and you deduct $3,000 from your taxable income. The government would probably need $6,000 to do the same amount of good the charity does more efficiently, so your $1,000 will do about $6,000 worth of good in your own community!

3. If all of us help those in need rather than depending on the government to do it, maybe our taxes could be reduced.

Keep a record of all the contributions that you make during the year on the "charitable contributions" form and save receipts for your donations in the "tax information" file. You or your accountant will need these to do your taxes.

Remember that giving to others helps us to overcome a major obstacle in our thinking about money—the fear of limited resources and the fear of letting go of our control over money. When we realize that we don't have to hoard our money, we experience a sense of financial freedom that is priceless.

Charitable Giving

Year _____

Date	Check Number	Charity	Amount
_____	_____	_____	_____
_____	_____	_____	_____
_____	_____	_____	_____
_____	_____	_____	_____
_____	_____	_____	_____
_____	_____	_____	_____
_____	_____	_____	_____
_____	_____	_____	_____
_____	_____	_____	_____
_____	_____	_____	_____
_____	_____	_____	_____
_____	_____	_____	_____
_____	_____	_____	_____
_____	_____	_____	_____
_____	_____	_____	_____
_____	_____	_____	_____
_____	_____	_____	_____
_____	_____	_____	_____
_____	_____	_____	_____
_____	_____	_____	_____
_____	_____	_____	_____
_____	_____	_____	_____
_____	_____	_____	_____
_____	_____	_____	_____
_____	_____	_____	_____
_____	_____	_____	_____

For your personal use, a copy of this form can be found in the back of this book.

EDUCATION
Your Best Investment

When we think of investments, we often think of stocks and bonds; but a far greater investment is in our education. Education not only gives us knowledge, but a liberal arts education also brings us an understanding and perspective that enriches our lives.

Education provides us with our earning power for a lifetime. It enables us to pursue our interests and talents and to develop our skills. Learn to do what you love to do with excellence. People will be willing to pay you when you serve a need and your heart is in it. Develop your talent; it will be the best investment you will ever make.

A good education does not have to be exorbitantly expensive—there are community colleges and in-state colleges that are very reasonable.

Note from the following chart how education affects income and your potential earning power. It reflects the difference that society is willing to pay you for your increased expertise.

How Education Affects Income
Age 25 or Older

Graduated Grade School	$15,043
1-3 Years High School	$18,298
Graduated High School	$31,376
1-3 Years of College	$37,156
Associate Degree	$42,118
Bachelor's Degree	$52,857
Master's Degree	$64,960
Professional Degree	$82,010

Be the best at what you do, and don't ever stop learning.

Keep a record of your school and work history in your binder using the forms in the back of this book. It is especially helpful when you are filling out job applications or writing a resume.

Be sure to keep the name and address of a reference for every job.

Invest in education for your children. Share your values and expose them to the tremendous opportunities of our free-enterprise system that is the envy of the world.

Open educational IRAs to which you can contribute $500/year if you make less than $95,000 ($150,000 if you are married). The earnings can be used tax-free for education, so start early and give them time to grow.

If your income is higher than the limits, you can open a Uniform Gifts to Minor Account or a Uniform Transfer to Minors Account. These are accounts that can appreciate to fund education, and the earnings are generally taxed at the child's lower bracket, with the first $700 income tax free. The disadvantage is that your child has control of these funds when they are 18 and 21 respectively. You may want to accumulate money in your own name, pay a bit more in taxes, and keep more control. (Check with your tax advisor or reference book for details.) Have your children participate in their education by working and saving money during the summers. Encourage them to study hard and to be active in leadership roles during the school year so they will be in a position to apply for scholarships and pursue the many avenues available for financial aid and low-interest loans.

Education

School _____

Address _____

_____

_____

Phone/Fax _____

Tuition _____

Years Attended _____

_____

Degree _____

_____

School _____

Address _____

_____

_____

Phone/Fax _____

Tuition _____

Years Attended _____

_____

Degree _____

_____

School _____

Address _____

_____

_____

Phone/Fax _____

Tuition _____

Years Attended _____

_____

Degree _____

School _____

Address _____

_____

_____

Phone/Fax _____

Tuition _____

Years Attended _____

_____

Degree _____

_____

School _____

Address _____

_____

_____

Phone/Fax _____

Tuition _____

Years Attended _____

_____

Degree _____

_____

School _____

Address _____

_____

_____

Phone/Fax _____

Tuition _____

Years Attended _____

_____

Degree _____

YOUR CAREER
Using Your Talents to Serve Others

Take some time to think about what you are being called to do with your life. What is your vocation? Do you feel called to be a spouse, a parent? What are your talents? We spend 35-60 hours or more a week working, so it makes sense to do what you love to do and get paid for it. If you find something you love to do, you'll never "work" another day in your life.

Consider owning your own business. Our free-enterprise, capitalistic system rewards efficient businesses that serve the needs of society. Owning your own business gives you free rein in decisions, creativity, many tax advantages, and the satisfaction of doing a job "your way." You take on the risk of failure but the potential for great financial reward.

There are major advantages but also disadvantages to consider. Do you want more time or more money? The advantages of owning your own business need to be weighed against the disadvantages of the full weight of a business on your shoulders. You give of your financial resources, your time and, most of all, your emotional energy.

It is becoming very important for women to prepare themselves with the skills necessary to be employed. The possibility of having to support yourself and your dependents due to death, disability, or divorce is increasing. Even if you choose to remain at home when your children are young, you never know when you may be called upon to support your family. You will feel much more secure knowing that you have some employable skill. Develop your hobbies and talents or take classes at a community college.

If you are both working when you get married, plan to live on one salary. Save and invest the second income. Then, when you decide to start a family, you will be prepared to live on one salary, and will have money accumulated for the added expense of a child.

Consider the value of one parent staying at home when your children are pre-school age. It is a precious, fleeting time when you have such a great influence on their values and development. Balance the costs of childcare, transportation, work clothes, and fast food, and you will realize you need to make a lot of money to make it financially worthwhile. And you may be giving up one of the greatest experiences of your life—time with your children.

Career

Whatever you choose to do, keep your work in perspective. Be open and share with one another the joys and frustrations of your work. It is also very important to have a working knowledge of your spouse's business affairs. You need to know who to call and what to do if something were to suddenly happen to your spouse.

Take time to appreciate how hard you both are working, whether at home or at the office. Take a few minutes each evening to share the best and the worst of your day—there are always blessings and concerns. Try to understand that a woman at home needs appreciation for her efforts, and a man who is working needs to find peace at home.

Job History/Resumé

Job History

Company _____

Years _____

Address _____

_____

_____

Phone _____

Reference _____

_____

_____

Company _____

Years _____

Address _____

_____

_____

Phone _____

Reference _____

_____

_____

Company _____

Years _____

Address _____

_____

_____

Phone _____

Reference _____

_____

_____

Company _____

Years _____

Address _____

_____

_____

Phone _____

Reference _____

_____

Professional Societies & Organizations

_____

_____

_____

_____

_____

_____

_____

_____

_____

_____

_____

_____

_____

_____

_____

_____

Research & Publications

_____

_____

_____

_____

_____

_____

_____

_____

_____

_____

Awards & Honors

_____

_____

_____

_____

_____

_____

_____

For your personal use, a copy of this form can be found in the back of this book.

MEDICAL/FAMILY
Health Makes Wealth

Invest in your physical, emotional, and mental well-being. Without your health, you cannot create wealth. Exercise, eat well, play as well as work, and take time for vacation, however you relax the most. It is not extravagant to take time off or take a family vacation; it is essential.

Family time and vacations don't have to be expensive. In fact, the best times often don't cost anything; consider a walk through the park, a picnic at sunset, or a vacation spent relaxing at home. Before and after children, be sure to keep a "date night" so you will always have time for one another. Make family time and time together as a couple a priority.

Financial planning must necessarily include a statement about your marriage and your family's health. If you are married, do everything you can to make your marriage the best it can be. Don't let money be a source of power in your relationship. Instead, be equals playing on the same team, bringing different strengths to your life together, sharing everything 50/50. Keep most of your property and accounts in joint ownership, but keep some individual investment accounts so money is being built up in both of your names.

We are all human, and no person or relationship is perfect. As you face the hurdles and challenges of life, especially when and if your financial problems seem overwhelming—get help. We all need advice and feedback from time to time, and there are many professionals through your church and community who can help you with your worst problems and fears.

Death, disability, and divorce can be devastating financially and emotionally, so take care of yourselves. While someone may come out better than the other, no one "wins" in a divorce, and the children are always the big losers. Do everything you can to work out your differences and rekindle the love that brought you together. If it is impossible, pray for the strength to still love, and to treat each other fairly and with compassion. It is a true measure of your character.

Use the forms in the back of the book to record information about your family, your doctors, medical claims, the dates of immunizations, and medical procedures.

Take the time to nurture your relationships with each other, your friends and family, your co-workers, the people you encounter every day, and especially your God.

In the end, these relationships make life worth living and bring us the greatest joy. This is the best place to invest your time, talent, and treasure.

Family Medical Information

Family Information

Name _____

Address _____

_____

_____

Phone _____

Phone (Work) _____

Fax _____

Soc. Sec. No. _____

Date of Birth _____

Place of Birth _____

Passport No. _____

Notes _____

Immunizations & Medical Notes

Physician _____

Address _____

Phone _____

Fax _____

Dentist _____

Address _____

Phone _____

Fax _____

Name _____

Address _____

_____

_____

Phone _____

Phone (Work) _____

Fax _____

Soc. Sec. No. _____

Date of Birth _____

Place of Birth _____

Passport No. _____

Notes _____

Physician _____

Address _____

Phone _____

Fax _____

Dentist _____

Address _____

Phone _____

Fax _____

Name _____

Address _____

_____

_____

Phone _____

Phone (Work) _____

Fax _____

Soc. Sec. No. _____

Date of Birth _____

Place of Birth _____

Passport No. _____

Notes _____

Physician _____

Address _____

Phone _____

Fax _____

Dentist _____

Address _____

Phone _____

Fax _____

Family Medical Information

Family Information

Name _____

Address _____

_____

_____

Phone _____

Phone (Work) _____

Fax _____

Soc. Sec. No. _____

Date of Birth _____

Place of Birth _____

Passport No. _____

Notes _____

_____

Immunizations & Medical Notes

Physician _____

Address _____

Phone _____

Fax _____

Dentist _____

Address _____

Phone _____

Fax _____

Name _____

Address _____

_____

_____

Phone _____

Phone (Work) _____

Fax _____

Soc. Sec. No. _____

Date of Birth _____

Place of Birth _____

Passport No. _____

Notes _____

_____

Physician _____

Address _____

Phone _____

Fax _____

Dentist _____

Address _____

Phone _____

Fax _____

Name _____

Address _____

_____

_____

Phone _____

Phone (Work) _____

Fax _____

Soc. Sec. No. _____

Date of Birth _____

Place of Birth _____

Passport No. _____

Notes _____

_____

Physician _____

Address _____

Phone _____

Fax _____

Dentist _____

Address _____

Phone _____

Fax _____

For your personal use, a copy of this form can be found in the back of this book.

Family Medical Information

Family Information

Immunizations & Medical Notes

Name _____

Address _____

_____

_____

Phone _____

Phone (Work) _____

Fax _____

Soc. Sec. No. _____

Date of Birth _____

Place of Birth _____

Passport No. _____

Notes _____

Physician _____

Address _____

_____

Phone _____

Fax _____

Dentist _____

Address _____

_____

Phone _____

Fax _____

Name _____

Address _____

_____

_____

Phone _____

Phone (Work) _____

Fax _____

Soc. Sec. No. _____

Date of Birth _____

Place of Birth _____

Passport No. _____

Notes _____

Physician _____

Address _____

_____

Phone _____

Fax _____

Dentist _____

Address _____

_____

Phone _____

Fax _____

Name _____

Address _____

_____

_____

Phone _____

Phone (Work) _____

Fax _____

Soc. Sec. No. _____

Date of Birth _____

Place of Birth _____

Passport No. _____

Notes _____

Physician _____

Address _____

_____

Phone _____

Fax _____

Dentist _____

Address _____

_____

Phone _____

Fax _____

Medical/Dental Payments

Name of Family Member and Doctor	Date of Visit	Amount of Charge	Amount Ins. Paid	Deductable Satified?		Co-Pay Amt. Paid	$ Paid out of Pocket
				YES	NO		
_____ _____	_____	_____	_____	❑	❑	_____	_____
_____ _____	_____	_____	_____	❑	❑	_____	_____
_____ _____	_____	_____	_____	❑	❑	_____	_____
_____ _____	_____	_____	_____	❑	❑	_____	_____
_____ _____	_____	_____	_____	❑	❑	_____	_____
_____ _____	_____	_____	_____	❑	❑	_____	_____
_____ _____	_____	_____	_____	❑	❑	_____	_____
_____ _____	_____	_____	_____	❑	❑	_____	_____
_____ _____	_____	_____	_____	❑	❑	_____	_____
_____ _____	_____	_____	_____	❑	❑	_____	_____

For your personal use, a copy of this form can be found in the back of this book.

BANK ACCOUNTS
Your "Peace of Mind" Fund

Now is the time to develop a great relationship with a banker—your personal banker. Go to several banks and check their types of accounts and the interest they pay you, their fees and services, but, most importantly, find someone with whom you feel comfortable working.

First, you will want to open a checking account for monthly expenses—check on fees, earnings, overdraft protection, and any minimum balances required. Share the responsibility of balancing your checkbook every month as soon as it arrives (or at least by the end of the week). Then, complete the income/expense sheet from chapter 3, and review together where your money was spent. If you need help balancing your checkbook, bank personnel are generally more than willing to show you how.

Open a separate money market account for an emergency fund. The money market account will pay you more interest than checking but will require a higher minimum balance and fewer monthly transactions. Accumulate cash in this account to cover three months of your expenses. That will provide the security you need for sudden emergencies and is a good investment for the good night's sleep it will give you. You will be able to self-insure for short-term disability (cover household expenses until your waiting period is over), and you won't have to depend on credit for unexpected events.

Apply for a line of credit at your bank once you meet the income, employment history, and credit rating requirements. The line of credit provides you with money you are authorized to borrow, if needed, and can augment your emergency fund.

If this authorization to borrow is secured by your home equity, the interest paid if you borrow may be (if you can itemize) tax deductible. You should have savings to cover three to six months of expenses accumulated in an emergency fund. If your monthly expenses are $2,000, you should have a minimum of $6,000 in savings and a $6,000 line of credit.

Banks are offering more and more financial services and, while the costs may be somewhat higher than other alternatives, when you are first starting out the simplicity of having your financial affairs at one place has value. Check to see if your money market account can be linked to a brokerage account, but be sure you understand the expenses associated with brokerage transactions. That way, money in excess of your emergency fund can regularly be invested. Open a safety deposit box for storing your valuables, and ask about other services including online access and Individual Retirement Accounts.

Bank Accounts

Name of Bank _____   **Notes:** _____

Address _____

_____

Bank's Web Address _____

Banker _____

Banker's E-mail _____

Phone _____

Fax _____

Account No. _____

_____

_____

_____

Access/ATM Card No. _____

Name of Bank _____   **Notes:** _____

Address _____

_____

Bank's Web Address _____

Banker _____

Banker's E-mail _____

Phone _____

Fax _____

Account No. _____

_____

_____

_____

Access/ATM Card No. _____

Name of Bank _____   **Notes:** _____

Address _____

_____

Bank's Web Address _____

Banker _____

Banker's E-mail _____

Phone _____

Fax _____

Account No. _____

_____

_____

_____

Access/ATM Card No. _____

For your personal use, a copy of this form can be found in the back of this book.

Bank Accounts

Name of Bank _____
Address _____
_____
Bank's Web Address _____
Banker _____
Banker's E-mail _____
Phone _____
Fax _____
Account No. _____
_____
_____
_____
Access/ATM Card No. _____

Notes: _____
_____
_____
_____
_____
_____
_____
_____
_____
_____
_____
_____
_____
_____

Name of Bank _____
Address _____
_____
Bank's Web Address _____
Banker _____
Banker's E-mail _____
Phone _____
Fax _____
Account No. _____
_____
_____
_____
Access/ATM Card No. _____

Notes: _____
_____
_____
_____
_____
_____
_____
_____
_____
_____
_____
_____
_____
_____

Name of Bank _____
Address _____
_____
Bank's Web Address _____
Banker _____
Banker's E-mail _____
Phone _____
Fax _____
Account No. _____
_____
_____
_____
Access/ATM Card No. _____

Notes: _____
_____
_____
_____
_____
_____
_____
_____
_____
_____
_____
_____
_____
_____

TRANSPORTATION
We Get Around

Usually, a car is our first serious investment. We are such a mobile society that a car is often a necessity. While it is ideal to buy outright, a short-term loan is justified since this use-asset transports us to and from our work, which is a money-generating activity.

Before buying an automobile, take advantage of the extensive information available at the library and on the Internet. Kelly Blue Book, Classifieds2000 on the Internet, and Consumer Reports are just a few of the many resources available.

Make safety your first priority. From a financial point of view, you have a lot to lose if you are disabled (or worse).

You can save a lot buying used cars, especially if you are mechanically inclined. If you are not mechanically inclined, it may be worthwhile to have a newer car still under warranty to keep maintenance costs low. It's also a good idea to buy a car that gets good mileage, you'll save money on gas, and it's better for the environment.

Look for a car with good resale value, that suits your lifestyle and that you really enjoy driving. It is a major investment that you will use every day, so make it special and something you will really appreciate. If you love your job, you love your family, and you love your car —every day will get off to a good start!

Keep records of car purchases and repairs in your binder, and keep the title of your car in your safety deposit box.

Car Information

Make and Model _____

Year_____

Purchase Date _____

Odometer Reading _____

Purchase Cost _____

Sales Tax_____

Title No._____

ID No. _____

Purchased From _____

Address _____

_____

_____

_____

Service Record

Who Performs Service _____

Service Phone No. _____

Major Repairs _____

_____

_____

_____

_____

_____

Contact _____

Phone No. _____

E-mail_____

Make and Model _____

Year_____

Purchase Date _____

Odometer Reading _____

Purchase Cost _____

Sales Tax_____

Title No._____

ID No. _____

Purchased From _____

Address _____

_____

_____

_____

Service Record

Who Performs Service _____

Service Phone No. _____

Major Repairs _____

_____

_____

_____

_____

_____

Contact _____

Phone No. _____

E-mail_____

Make and Model _____

Year_____

Purchase Date _____

Odometer Reading _____

Purchase Cost _____

Sales Tax_____

Title No._____

ID No. _____

Purchased From _____

Address _____

_____

_____

_____

Service Record

Who Performs Service _____

Service Phone No. _____

Major Repairs _____

_____

_____

_____

_____

_____

Contact _____

Phone No. _____

E-mail_____

REAL ESTATE
Home is Where the Heart Is

It is part of the American dream to own your own home. Your home can be an excellent investment for you: the interest on your loan and the property taxes you pay are tax deductible, the value of your home will generally increase over the years, and the profit you make when you sell your home is often tax exempt.

The question is not if you should purchase a home but when. To determine whether you should rent or buy, consider the following questions.

Will you be living in the area for at least three years? While real estate historically appreciates about 4% per year, closing costs and loan fees usually make it unprofitable to sell sooner than this.

Do you want the freedom to move quickly if a better job opportunity presents itself?

Have you saved up enough for a down payment (10% to 20% of the cost)?

Can you afford the maintenance, utilities, property taxes, and insurance you will need to pay as well as the mortgage payment?

While home ownership may be a definite long-term goal, you may enjoy the flexibility and freedom of not being tied to the responsibility and cost of a home initially. The money you can afford for housing when you are first married may provide for a very nice apartment but may not be enough to provide for a very nice home.

When you are in the position to buy your first home, consider home ownership in steps. Rather than buying the biggest house you can qualify for at the bank and then being burdened by large mortgage payments, buy an affordable home for your current budget. Then, in about five years as your needs change, sell and use the profit for the down payment on a new home that fits your budget and changing lifestyle.

When you are ready to purchase a home, it can be an excellent investment, and it is one of the last tax havens available.

If you are in the position to itemize, you can lower your tax liability by deducting the interest you pay on your loan, whereas rent payments are just money out the window.

The value of your home will probably appreciate over the years, so it is a working asset. As this asset increases, your liability (home mortgage) decreases, thereby increasing your net worth. If you can afford it, consider a vacation home for the same benefits.

Your home is your retreat, and it is the environment in which you live out your life with your loved ones.

It is a use-asset that you can enjoy every day. It is an appreciating asset, and the interest you pay is tax-deductible. I'd say that is a great investment!

Remember the three rules for buying real estate: LOCATION—LOCATION—LOCATION.

It is much better to buy the worst house in the best neighborhood than the best home in a bad neighborhood. Get an appraisal, an inspection, and legal advice before you buy anything.

Owning rental property has similar benefits if you don't mind the management headaches.

Record information concerning real estate purchases and improvements. You or your accountant will need this information at the end of the year, and you will need this for future reference if you sell your home.

There is also a page in this section to record a list of your home inventory and information about major purchases and warranties.

It is advisable to have a video or pictorial record of your possessions in your safety deposit box in the event of a property loss.

Consider putting your photo negatives in the back of your freezer to preserve them. Whenever a home burns down and people lose all their possessions, the pictures—those cherished memories—are usually the thing they most regret losing.

Real Estate Information

Date of Purchase _____   Address _____

Purchase Price _____   _____

Date of Sale _____   _____

Selling Price _____   _____

Home Information

Date	Improvement	Cost

Keep a copy of your closing statement and receipts from all major purchases and improvements, which add to the value of your home.

Home Inventory

Major purchases	Date	Cost	Serial #	Warranty

Other: _____

_____

_____

_____

_____

_____

_____

_____

_____

_____

_____

_____

_____

_____

INSURANCE
Cover Your Assets

Insurance is not an investment but protection against the loss of the assets you are building. Insurance is important for catastrophes, so set your maximum limits high. You may be able to handle a $500 bill for damage to your home but not its replacement if it burns down.

To keep your premiums lower, get the highest deductibles you can afford and the longest waiting periods ($1,000 deductibles on auto and 90-day waits on disability can dramatically lower your rates). You will pay less out for insurance coverage and you won't have to make small claims that will increase your premiums. You can self-insure, using your emergency fund, to pay small claims, to cover a deductible, or to pay bills during the waiting period if you become disabled. Shop around for low premiums. Many times premiums are lower when you buy more than one policy from a company.

Make sure you are covered for

Automobile insurance: The law requires coverage for collision, and liability for all drivers and modes of transportation. If your car is a major asset, you will want comprehensive coverage. If your car is paid for, and not worth a lot, comprehensive isn't required.

Renters or homeowners insurance: Whether you rent or own your home, you need coverage on all your furnishings and personal property. If you own your home, you also need to cover the replacement value of your home and liability for accidents on your property. Compare premiums. The policies offered through your mortgage company are sometimes required but can be more expensive.

Medical insurance: If you can get family medical coverage from your employer, it is a great benefit. Otherwise, it will pay to shop around, get a high deductible, high maximum coverage, and stay healthy. Watch out for low first-year premiums followed by excessive increases. Keep in mind that if your health changes, insurance coverage can be difficult, if not impossible, to obtain. There is a benefit to getting a good policy, with limited potential premium increases and not changing policies too often.

Life insurance: If you are both working, you do not need life insurance. Your emergency fund can help with funeral expenses and transition, and you can continue to work. Once you have someone dependent on you, look for term, not whole life, insurance. Term coverage will give you the protection you need. The money you save by not buying expensive whole life policies can be invested on your own for better returns.

Disability insurance: This is as important as life insurance once you have someone dependent on you, you have built up your financial assets, you have significant monthly payments, and only one of you is working. But it can be expensive. A longer waiting period will drastically reduce premiums. Try to self-insure for the first 90 days using your emergency fund. It is advisable to purchase the maximum coverage (usually 50% of earnings), own-occupation coverage (which covers your particular line of work), and an inflation rider so your coverage increases over the years to keep up with inflation.

Liability insurance: This is often included in automobile and homeowners insurance. Look for $100,000/$300,000 liability limits at a minimum.

Umbrella liability insurance: This inexpensive insurance gives you liability coverage above your basic coverage. It is a worthwhile policy to have as your net worth increases or you are at risk of being sued.

Long-term care insurance: This can be very expensive, but as you get older, if you are concerned about being dependent on others, you may want to consider this for peace of mind.

For your records, keep a basic summary of all your policies for easy reference.

Insurance

Automobile

Company _____ Policy # _____

Address _____ Agent _____

_____ Phone # _____

Coverage _____

_____ Cost _____

Homeowners

Company _____ Policy # _____

Address _____ Agent _____

_____ Phone # _____

Coverage _____

_____ Cost _____

Medical

Company _____ Policy # _____

Address _____ Agent _____

_____ Phone # _____

Coverage _____

_____ Cost _____

Life

Company _____ Policy # _____

Address _____ Agent _____

_____ Phone # _____

Coverage _____

_____ Cost _____

Disability

Company _____ Policy # _____

Address _____ Agent _____

_____ Phone # _____

Coverage _____

_____ Cost _____

Liability

Company _____ Policy # _____

Address _____ Agent _____

_____ Phone # _____

Coverage _____

_____ Cost _____

For your personal use, a copy of this form can be found in the back of this book.

Other Insurance

Type of Insurance _____

Company _____ Policy # _____

Address _____ Agent _____

_____ Phone # _____

Coverage _____

_____ Cost _____

Type of Insurance _____

Company _____ Policy # _____

Address _____ Agent _____

_____ Phone # _____

Coverage _____

_____ Cost _____

Type of Insurance _____

Company _____ Policy # _____

Address _____ Agent _____

_____ Phone # _____

Coverage _____

_____ Cost _____

Type of Insurance _____

Company _____ Policy # _____

Address _____ Agent _____

_____ Phone # _____

Coverage _____

_____ Cost _____

Type of Insurance _____

Company _____ Policy # _____

Address _____ Agent _____

_____ Phone # _____

Coverage _____

_____ Cost _____

Type of Insurance _____

Company _____ Policy # _____

Address _____ Agent _____

_____ Phone # _____

Coverage _____

_____ Cost _____

COMPOUNDING INTEREST
The Eighth Wonder of the World

%

Understanding the concept of compounding interest is essential to building your financial future. It opens your eyes to the possibility of phenomenal growth. It illustrates the way money appreciates and how you can make your money work for you. It demonstrates that the more you invest for the future, the more you win, and the more you live on credit, the more you lose.

Keep in mind the "Rule of 72," which states that if you divide 72 by the interest rate you hope to earn, the result will be the number of years it will take your investment to DOUBLE!

If you have $5,000 invested at 4%, it will double every 18 years (72 divided by 4 = 18).

$5,000 invested at 8% will double every 9 years (72 divided by 8 = 9)

$5,000 invested at 12% will double every 6 years (72 divided by 12 = 6). So in 18 years:

$5,000 at 4% compounds to $10,000

$5,000 at 8% compounds to $20,000

$5,000 at 12% compounds to $40,000

When you invest your money, your money is growing and working for you. When you borrow money, this same principle—the Rule of 72—works against you.

You may be familiar with the concept of compounding interest if you have ever paid down a loan. For example, if you have a 15-year $100,000 home loan at 9%, you will have paid $305,500 when the loan is paid off. Wouldn't you like to receive that kind of growth rather than the bank?

In the following chapters, we will explore how compounding interest works for you in retirement and investment accounts and against you with credit cards and loans. This distinction is key to financial success and peace of mind.

RETIREMENT
Let Your Money Work for You

The greatest benefit of compounding interest can be utilized in retirement accounts.

Retirement accounts offer the advantages of often being tax deductible or untaxed income, with the appreciation and reinvested earnings tax deferred until you take them out at retirement. At that point you will most likely be in a lower tax bracket.

Retirement accounts right now offer us the very best financial investments we can possibly make—and the earlier you start, the greater, by far, the benefits you will reap.

The exciting benefits of compound interest are shown on the chart on the next page. If you start at age 22 to put $2,000 each year into an IRA and just invest a total of $18,000 over the next 9 years, even if you stop contributing at age 30, your money in your account will accumulate to $763,000 by the time you reach 65!

If you wait to start until you are 31 and put in $2,000 each year for 35 years (a total of $70,000), you will accumulate $542,000 by the time you are 65. The person who starts at age 22 contributes less and accumulates more!

Even better, if you contribute throughout your lifetime (from age 22 to age 65), you will have almost $1.3 million (in today's dollars) at retirement!

Start with a Roth IRA. It is not tax deductible, but the earnings are not taxed even when you take money out. This opportunity phases out as your income increases. Then you need to invest in a regular IRA or a SEP, Keogh, profit sharing, 401(k), or any other plan your employer may have.

Retirement

Individual Retirement Account at 10% Total Return

Age	Contributions Made Early	Contributions Made Later	Contributions Made Continuously
22	$2,000	.0	$2,000
23	2,000	.0	2,000
24	2,000	.0	2,000
25	2,000	.0	2,000
26	2,000	.0	2,000
27	2,000	.0	2,000
28	2,000	.0	2,000
29	2,000	.0	2,000
30	2,000	.0	2,000
31	.0	$2,000	2,000
32	.0	2,000	2,000
33	.0	2,000	2,000
34	.0	2,000	2,000
35	.0	2,000	2,000
36	.0	2,000	2,000
37	.0	2,000	2,000
38	.0	2,000	2,000
39	.0	2,000	2,000
40	.0	2,000	2,000
41	.0	2,000	2,000
42	.0	2,000	2,000
43	.0	2,000	2,000
44	.0	2,000	2,000
45	.0	2,000	2,000
46	.0	2,000	2,000
47	.0	2,000	2,000
48	.0	2,000	2,000
49	.0	2,000	2,000
50	.0	2,000	2,000
51	.0	2,000	2,000
52	.0	2,000	2,000
53	.0	2,000	2,000
54	.0	2,000	2,000
55	.0	2,000	2,000
56	.0	2,000	2,000
57	.0	2,000	2,000
58	.0	2,000	2,000
59	.0	2,000	2,000
60	.0	2,000	2,000
61	.0	2,000	2,000
62	.0	2,000	2,000
63	.0	2,000	2,000
64	.0	2,000	2,000
65	.0	2,000	2,000
Amount Available at Age 65	**$763,000**	**$542,000**	**$1,305,000**

Total of $18,000 Invested

Total of $70,000 Invested

Total of $88,000 Invested

A retirement plan through your employer is a wonderful benefit and adds significantly to your compensation. Find out the details of your plan. Ask about the vesting schedule (how long you need to stay to receive the employer's full contribution). If your employer matches funds, maximize this benefit fully. Ask about investment alternatives. Since these are long-term investments, I recommend that retirement funds be invested in growth stock mutual funds whenever you have the choice, since they have great potential for high total return over time. If you change employment, avoid the heavy penalties of cashing out your retirement account, by rolling it over to an IRA or a new retirement account. Try not to borrow against your retirement account, even though that is allowable under certain circumstances like education or a first mortgage. You really want that money growing exponentially.

How much should you save for retirement? Generally, you can assume that in retirement you will want about 80% of your current income before retirement. There are many books and software programs that can help you set a goal based on your age, income, years to retirement, assumed inflation, and earnings rate on your investments.

Basically, the steps are to:

Figure annual retirement income desired (80% current income) and reduce by Social Security expected (you can call the Social Security office at 1-800-772-1213 for a projection of that annual benefit) to determine how much you will need from savings and investments. Multiply this number by how many years you plan to live in retirement.

Calculate the future value of what you have already saved through retirement accounts and other investments. The difference will be what you will need to accumulate. Computer programs can help you determine how much you need to save annually to reach your goal.

The important thing to remember is to start now and fully fund any accounts available to you. As soon as you have earned income, open a retirement account and get your money working for you. Then you will enjoy the fruits of your planning when you are ready to retire. It is the key to maintaining your quality of life when you no longer choose to work.

Here is a summary of various retirement accounts

Profit-sharing plan

◆ Up to 15% of salary contributed by employer on behalf of employee

◆ Usually based on annual profits—no guarantee on contribution

◆ Vesting schedule with increasing percentage with years of service

Pension

◆ Employer contributes, some plans employees contribute

◆ Defined benefit guarantees a specific payment at retirement

◆ Defined contribution—specific amount contributed—earnings vary

401(k)

◆ Your pre-tax contribution reduces taxable income

◆ Matching contributions optional

◆ A percentage up to $10,000 of salary

◆ Self-directed-optional investment opportunities

403(b)

◆ For non-profit employees

◆ Up to 20% of pre-tax salary, $10,000 limit for 1998

SIMPLE

◆ For businesses with less than 100 employees

◆ Matching contributions

Thrift Plan

◆ Federal employees

◆ Matching optional

Section 457

◆ State employees; no matching

SEP-IRA

◆ Simplified employee pension plans

◆ Small-business owners and self-employed

◆ Tax deductible contributions—earnings tax-deferred

◆ Percentage of income (up to $22,500)

◆ Simple and flexible

Roth IRA

◆ Contributions not deductible

◆ Income limits: $150,000–$160,000 married; $95,000–$110,000, single.

◆ If you hold for 5 years, no penalty for withdrawals of contributions

◆ Earnings not taxed at retirement

Traditional IRA

◆ $2,000 limit (with earned income)

◆ Deductible with income limits

◆ Earnings tax-deferred

Keogh

◆ For self-employed; $30,000 maximum, or up to 25% of earnings

◆ Must match for employees; earnings tax-deferred

Annuities

◆ Tax-deferred earnings; no cap on contributions

◆ Fixed annuities—offers guaranteed income stream

◆ Variable annuities—offers investment alternatives

◆ Some have high fees and expenses

◆ Regular tax vs. capital gain

Retirement

Name of Account _____

Policy # _____

Phone _____

Fax _____

E-mail _____

Agent _____

Company _____

Address _____

Date _____

Beneficiary _____

Terms—vesting schedule _____

_____

_____

Name of Account _____

Policy # _____

Phone _____

Fax _____

E-mail _____

Agent _____

Company _____

Address _____

Date _____

Beneficiary _____

Terms—vesting schedule _____

_____

_____

Name of Account _____

Policy # _____

Phone _____

Fax _____

E-mail _____

Agent _____

Company _____

Address _____

Date _____

Beneficiary _____

Terms—vesting schedule _____

_____

_____

CREDIT IS CRAZY
You Work Hard for the Money

While credit cards can be beneficial for emergencies and to establish a good credit history, they have resulted in people living way beyond their means and accumulating debt that is far beyond their ability to budget. They are a major source of stress to any couple.

The major apprehension I have encountered with young couples is an uneasiness about credit. Usually one person has credit-card debt and the other one is concerned but uncomfortable about bringing up a possible conflict. You have to communicate about debt, resolve differences, and commit to living within your means in order to have financial peace in your relationships.

When you buy on credit, your money is working for the credit-card company and you are paying a hefty premium on everything you buy. Don't be a credit junkie. If you can't pay for it up front, you don't need it yet. If you really want something, let your money accumulate with interest and buy that particular item outright. You can survive six months to a year without, and you will appreciate your purchases more when you have saved up for them.

It used to be much more difficult to get a credit card. Now young people are being extended so much credit that they become quickly enslaved to repayments for years. Don't get trapped into letting the credit-card companies make their millions off of you.

Remember the "rule of 72." Divide 72 by the interest rate you pay to determine how long it will take for your cost to double.

If you borrow $5,000 at 18% (like most credit cards), and pay it off in 4 years, your purchase will actually cost you double—or $10,000! (72 divided by 18 = 4.)

If you are in credit-card debt now or in the future, don't despair—just resolve to turn it around. Look at what you owe now. How soon can you pay it off? Six months or one year? Good—just do it! That is the best financial step you can make. Pay off cards with the highest interest rate first. Consider consolidating to one credit card with lower fees and interest or a debt-consolidation loan. If you find you cannot pay off your credit cards within one year or are in serious credit debt, contact the consumer credit bureau in your city and they may be able to help you satisfy your creditors and get you back on track.

It is very important to keep an excellent credit rating and to realize that your credit information is available and shared between many institutions. Be sure to pay your bills on time: credit cards, rent, mortgages, car payments.

Don't open more credit accounts than you need. Each one indicates another inquiry on your credit and provides more potential for debt.

Periodically request a copy of your credit report to make sure there are no mistakes and that you are maintaining an excellent credit rating. If you are ever turned down for credit, you can request a free report to find out why and correct the problem.

One of the wisest steps you can take to improve your financial situation is to pay off credit-card debt and never charge anything that you cannot pay back without interest. The first time you cannot pay a credit card bill without paying interest charges, take some scissors and cut the card up, throw it away, and promise not to use one again.

Credit Is Crazy

Credit Cards

Credit Card Company _____   **Notes:** _____
Account No. _____   _____
Phone_____   _____
Name on Card _____   _____
Interest Rate _____   _____

Credit Card Company _____   **Notes:** _____
Account No. _____   _____
Phone_____   _____
Name on Card _____   _____
Interest Rate _____   _____

Credit Card Company _____   **Notes:** _____
Account No. _____   _____
Phone_____   _____
Name on Card _____   _____
Interest Rate _____   _____

Credit Card Company _____   **Notes:** _____
Account No. _____   _____
Phone_____   _____
Name on Card _____   _____
Interest Rate _____   _____

Credit Card Company _____   **Notes:** _____
Account No. _____   _____
Phone_____   _____
Name on Card _____   _____
Interest Rate _____   _____

Credit Card Company _____   **Notes:** _____
Account No. _____   _____
Phone_____   _____
Name on Card _____   _____
Interest Rate _____   _____

Credit Card Company _____   **Notes:** _____
Account No. _____   _____
Phone_____   _____
Name on Card _____   _____
Interest Rate _____   _____

For your personal use, a copy of this form can be found in the back of this book.

LOANS
The Real Cost of Borrowing Money

Loans, like credit cards, illustrate the negative effect of compounding interest. With loans, the lending institution is making the money at your expense. Remember, whenever possible, you are better off saving up and then purchasing rather than buying on credit and paying interest. For major purchases, however, loans may be necessary.

Car Loans

Consider the possibility of buying a used car or a cost-efficient car with no loan if you can do the maintenance yourself. If you prefer to purchase a new car with a warranty or need to finance your purchase, look for the lowest interest rate (often dealers have very low rates) and pay off your loan as quickly as possible, at least within 36 months. Car leases for personal use are rarely a good investment, but could be considered for business use.

Educational loans

Educational loans are important because a good education is a priority, not only to your earning potential but also for enhancing every aspect of your life. Look for good values in schools; many colleges offer scholarships and excellent courses at reasonable prices. Shop around for low-interest education loans, and check to see if your employer will support you in furthering your education.

Home mortgage

Work toward the goal of having only one loan—a home mortgage—and plan to have that paid off before retirement. You do not have to live in a mansion to be happy. Find a home that suits your family's needs, but also fits your budget.

Home Mortgage Considerations

Assumptions:

1. $50,000 gross income, interest rate 7%

2. Loan expense cannot exceed 28% of income = $1,167/month

3. Loan & other debt cannot exceed 36% of income = $1,583/month

— With No Debt

Can qualify for $175,000 loan, payment at $1,200/month

— With $500/Month in Other Debt

Can qualify for $115,000 loan, payment at $1,000/month

— With $1,000/Month in Other Debt

Can qualify for $57,000 loan, payment at $500/month

If you choose a home for $100,000 (2 x gross income) or less, you can see that if you eliminate all other debt you will be comfortable with your payments.

If you go for the largest house you can afford and then take on any other debts, it may be difficult to meet all your payments.

The amount you will qualify to borrow is based on a percentage of your monthly income and the amount of debt you already have. Don't go for the maximum you can borrow, because if you have to take on other debt it may be difficult to meet all your payments. You may need to start with a 30-year loan to afford the lower payments. If at all possible, apply for or convert to a 15-year loan. You will save a tremendous amount of interest and have your home paid off in half the time.

Shop around for a low fixed rate, or a variable rate that has a ceiling limiting how much it can increase. Allocate monthly what you will have to pay in property taxes and maintenance. Try not to let your house payment exceed 25% of your income so stress will not limit your enjoyment.

Keep in mind that your mortgage interest is fully deductible if you itemize (up to a $1,000,000 debt). Business interest is deductible with some limitations, but interest on other loans and credit cards is not deductible.

Keep track of your total debt payments as a percentage of your gross income. It should never exceed 35% and should decrease over the years.

Pray and communicate before any major investment. Whenever you commit to a loan, you are committing yourself to working to pay that debt and that limits your sense of financial freedom. Only make major investment choices when you both agree that the quality of life will be enhanced. Then you will really enjoy both your work and the fruits of your labor.

Mortgage Amortizations

Assumptions:
1. Loan Amount $50,000
2. Interest Rate 7%

	15-Year Loan	**30-Year Loan**
Monthly Payments	$450	$333
Interest Paid Over Period of Loan	$31,000	$70,000
Sum of All Payments	$81,000	$120,000
Equity in Home After 15 Years	100%	26%
	Fully Owned	Ownership $13,000 of Principal Paid

For $117 more a month over 15 years, you save almost $40,000 in interest and have full ownership of your home in 15 years.

Loans

Original Loan Amount _____

Date	Interest Rate	Balance	Payment

Home Mortgage _____ ____ _____ _____ _____

Bank _____

Contact _____   Notes _____

Address _____   _____

_____ _____

E-mail _____ _____

Phone/Fax _____ _____

Loan # _____ _____

Original Loan Amount _____

Date	Interest Rate	Balance	Payment

Second Mortgage _____ ____ _____ _____ _____

Bank _____

Contact _____   Notes _____

Address _____ _____

_____ _____

E-mail _____ _____

Phone/Fax _____ _____

Loan # _____ _____

Original Loan Amount _____

Date	Interest Rate	Balance	Payment

Automobile _____ ____ _____ _____ _____

Bank _____

Contact _____   Notes _____

Address _____ _____

_____ _____

E-mail _____ _____

Phone/Fax _____ _____

Loan # _____ _____

Original Loan Amount _____

Date	Interest Rate	Balance	Payment

Second Automobile _____ ____ _____ _____ _____

Bank _____

Contact _____   Notes _____

Address _____ _____

_____ _____

E-mail _____ _____

Phone/Fax _____ _____

Loan # _____ _____

Loans

Original Balance _____

Date	Interest Rate	Balance	Payment

Other Loans _____

Bank _____

Contact _____ Notes _____

Address _____ _____

_____ _____

E-mail _____ _____

Phone/Fax _____ _____

Loan # _____ _____

Original Balance _____

Date	Interest Rate	Balance	Payment

Other Loans _____

Bank _____

Contact _____ Notes _____

Address _____ _____

_____ _____

E-mail _____ _____

Phone/Fax _____ _____

Loan # _____ _____

Original Balance _____

Date	Interest Rate	Balance	Payment

Other Loans _____

Bank _____

Contact _____ Notes _____

Address _____ _____

_____ _____

E-mail _____ _____

Phone/Fax _____ _____

Loan # _____ _____

Original Balance _____

Date	Interest Rate	Balance	Payment

Other Loans _____

Bank _____

Contact _____ Notes _____

Address _____ _____

_____ _____

E-mail _____ _____

Phone/Fax _____ _____

Loan # _____ _____

INVESTMENTS
How to Reach Your Goals

After you have the fundamentals in place—emergency fund, bank accounts, car, home, insurance, loans, retirement, and charitable giving—congratulate yourselves. You have accomplished so much. Time for a vacation or at least a night out!

Now you are at a point to begin an investment plan, which will make any surplus money work for you. Before you invest, it is important to understand and implement some basic principles concerning risk and rewards of investment choices.

Purchasing power risk

There are many people who procrastinate when it comes to investing because they feel it is too risky. Because of inflation, it is too risky NOT to invest. Remember the rule of 72? If inflation is 3%, it will take 24 years for the cost of a product to double. If you have $1,000 today and bury it in the ground for 24 years, you will only be able to buy $500 worth of goods. You lose! If you had invested that money with a 9% return, you would have $8,000 to spend. There is more risk in doing nothing than in doing something—so you need to determine your risk tolerance and do something.

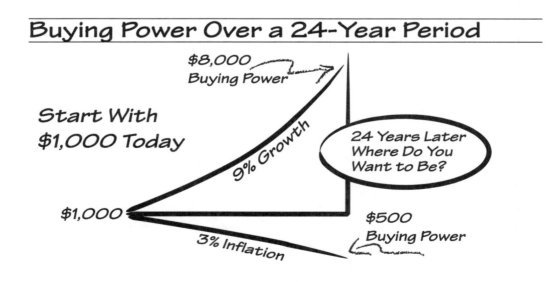

Buying Power Over a 24-Year Period

Start With $1,000 Today

$8,000 Buying Power

9% Growth

24 Years Later Where Do You Want to Be?

$1,000

3% Inflation

$500 Buying Power

Investment Alternatives

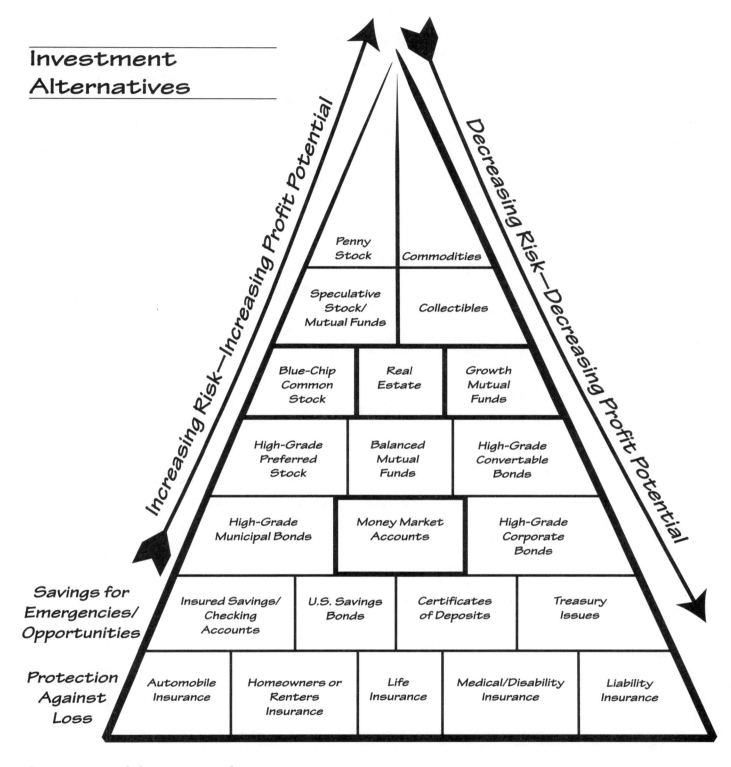

Increasing Risk—Increasing Profit Potential

Decreasing Risk—Decreasing Profit Potential

| Penny Stock | Commodities |

| Speculative Stock/ Mutual Funds | Collectibles |

| Blue-Chip Common Stock | Real Estate | Growth Mutual Funds |

| High-Grade Preferred Stock | Balanced Mutual Funds | High-Grade Convertable Bonds |

| High-Grade Municipal Bonds | Money Market Accounts | High-Grade Corporate Bonds |

Savings for Emergencies/ Opportunities

| Insured Savings/ Checking Accounts | U.S. Savings Bonds | Certificates of Deposits | Treasury Issues |

Protection Against Loss

| Automobile Insurance | Homeowners or Renters Insurance | Life Insurance | Medical/Disability Insurance | Liability Insurance |

Investment risk vs. reward

This chart shows various investment alternatives. Those at the bottom of the pyramid have the least risk of loss of principle but the lowest reward potential; those at the top have the highest risk and volatility but possible high returns. The goal is to find your comfort level so you get the highest return and still have a good night's sleep.

The chart to the right indicates the historical returns on different types of investments. You will note that the investment at the top will barely keep up with inflation.

Probable Investment Returns Over Long-Term Periods

(30 Years) for Various Investments

	Compounded Annual Return
Inflation	2 - 4%
Gold, Silver, etc.	2 - 4%
Treasury Bills, CDs, Cash Equivalents	3 - 5%
Annuities & Cash Value Life Insurance (Fixed)	4 - 6%
Long-Term Government Bonds	5 - 7%
Long-Term Corporate Bonds	6 - 8%
Annuities & Cash Value Life Insurance (Variable)	6 - 8%
Income-Producing Commercial Real Estate	8 - 10%
Large Company Stocks	9 - 12%
Small Company Stocks	10 - 13%

The second chart shows how much more you can accumulate over time with just a small increase in percentage return because of compounding interest.

Don't take on more risk than you are comfortable with, or you will sell out at exactly the wrong time. On the other hand, if you take on too little risk, you will earn far less than you potentially could. Which brings us to asset allocation.

Let Your Money Work for You:

Investing a $10,000 Lump-Sum Amount

Interest Earned	10 Years	30 Years
5%	$16,289	$43,219
6%	17,908	57,435
7%	19,672	76,123
8%	21,589	100,627
9%	23,674	132,677
10%	25,937	174,494
11%	28,394	228,923
12%	31,058	299,599

Asset Allocation

Based on how much risk you feel comfortable with and how comfortable you are riding the fluctuations of the market for better returns, determine where your money should be invested. Generally the younger you are and the longer you have until you need your money, the more risk you can take. When you are young, invest a greater percentage of your money in index funds, growth funds, small and mid-cap business funds, international funds, and emerging market funds. As you approach retirement, shift a larger percentage toward blue-chip funds, individual stocks, intermediate bond funds, and cash as needed. If you feel finan-

Allocating Your Assets
Based On Risk Personality

	Conservative	Moderate	Aggressive
Cash	20%	15%	10%
Bonds	25%	15%	10%
Stocks	55%	70%	80%

cially secure, continue to invest in growth for the money you will pass on to future generations. Now that is looking ahead.

Market risk—Variable vs. Fixed Returns (Lending vs. Owning)

With interest-bearing accounts, such as bank accounts, certificates of deposit, and bonds, you lend your money to businesses and they pay you back your principal plus interest. Since your principal is assured, these accounts are appropriate for emergency funds and monies that will be needed in the near future.

When you invest in stocks or stock funds you are buying part of the company, and your principal has the opportunity to grow as well as dividends increasing. Our free-enterprise, capitalistic society rewards businesses that efficiently serve the needs of society and, by owning part of the businesses we believe in, we share in the profits.

Historically, stocks fluctuate over the long term; however they far exceed interest-bearing accounts in growth, and ultimately, purchasing power. The chart at the top of the next page demonstrates the dramatic difference between the growth of stocks and bonds.

When you reach retirement, you will be glad you chose to be an owner and not a lender.

Stocks Versus Bonds
(Owning Versus Lending)

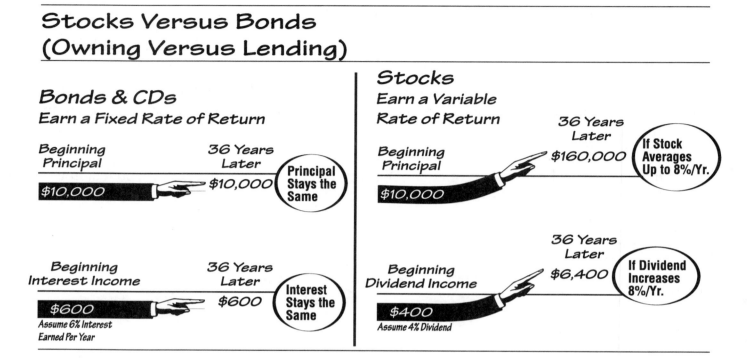

Bonds & CDs
Earn a Fixed Rate of Return

Beginning Principal

$10,000

36 Years Later

$10,000

Principal Stays the Same

Beginning Interest Income

$600

Assume 6% Interest Earned Per Year

36 Years Later

$600

Interest Stays the Same

Stocks
Earn a Variable Rate of Return

Beginning Principal

$10,000

36 Years Later

$160,000

If Stock Averages Up to 8%/Yr.

Beginning Dividend Income

$400

Assume 4% Dividend

36 Years Later

$6,400

If Dividend Increases 8%/Yr.

Diversification

Diversification means spreading your investments around. You already have diversification if you have an emergency fund (cash), own your own home (real estate), and a retirement fund (hopefully in growth stocks).

But where do you begin when you want to buy stocks in your personal portfolio? Because even the best companies will have their ups and downs, it is important not to put all your eggs in one basket. That is why it is wise to invest initially in mutual funds. Mutual funds pool the money of many investors and employ professional managers to buy shares of many different stocks to achieve specific goals. A total index fund purchased directly from the fund is the least expensive way to get into the market and maintain diversification. This provides you with ownership of many stocks across the board. Index funds are not actively traded, reducing tax consequences and commissions, and fees are low—so the return is hard to beat even by proficient money managers.

As you have more money to invest, and as you increase your knowledge and skills, you may want to look into a variety of specialty funds or individual stocks. Remember that mutual funds that trade a lot will cost you in transaction costs, as well as taxes on capital gains and dividends, so they would be more suited to retirement accounts with deferred taxation. In your personal portfolios you will eventually want to look for individual stocks with lower dividends and greater growth potential. Also look for companies you want to hold for the long term. Less trading postpones taxes on capital gains until you decide to sell.

Morningstar for mutual funds and Value Line for stocks are excellent publications, both available at the library, that present detailed descriptions and comparisons of most mutual funds and stocks.

Look for stocks that have consistently performed well over the past three to five years, in good years and in bad—not the hot performers of the past twelve months, which have already peaked. Have all dividends reinvested through an automatic reinvestment plan whenever possible.

Also look for value indicated by low price-to-earnings ratios and low relative price-earnings ratios. Use your expertise and search for companies in areas you understand that are well-managed, high-quality, and leaders in their industries.

Costs

To increase your return, keep your costs low. Buy no-load mutual funds directly from the fund, buy online, or buy stocks through discount brokers.

Buy companies you believe in that have a product people will need in the future, and hold for the long term, reducing trading commissions and capital gains taxes.

If you feel more comfortable with a broker handling your account, look for a fee-only Certified Financial Planner. They do not take commissions on their recommendations to you. If you are working with a broker, be sure to understand and compare commissions and management fees, which can reduce your total return.

Dollar-Cost Average

Finally, spread your investments out over time and invest at regular intervals, weekly, monthly, annually, whether the market is up or down. If possible, have a certain amount deducted from each paycheck and sent directly to your investment account. If the market is up, your $100 may only buy 4 shares at $25. When the market is low, you may buy 5 shares at $20 so your average cost per share is $22.22. You end up buying more shares at the lower rate and it averages out to your advantage. Don't try to time the market—it just does not work.

MUTUAL FUNDS SUMMARY AND DEFINITIONS

Benefits

Diversification of investments

Professional management

Convenience of buying, selling, transfers

Reinvestment options

Types of funds

Index funds—follow a market index; low fees

Tax-free funds—municipal securities, state tax-exempt

Aggressive growth funds—high-risk growth stocks

Growth funds—more established companies, growth expectations

Small company growth funds—smaller companies with predicted growth

Growth and income funds—growth plus significant dividend income

Income funds—bonds and stocks paying large dividends

Balanced funds—bonds, preferred stock, and common stock

Bond funds—invest in government and corporate bonds

International funds—overseas markets

Global funds—overseas and U.S. securities

Money market funds—short-term interest instruments

Definitions

Load—You pay fees plus a commission when you buy or sell

No-load—no commissions but usually fees

Open-end—fund grows with additional investments

Closed-end—fixed number of shares traded on major exchanges

NAV (Net asset value)—cost of one share

The Major Indexes

Dow Jones Industrial Index—The 30 stocks which make up this well-known average only represent a small percent of the total issues, but because they are the largest companies they contribute about one-third of the total market value and are considered good indicators of market trends.

Standard and Poor's 500 Index—The 500 companies represented in this index are considered to be the leading companies in leading industries in the U.S. economy and represent about 93% of the total market value of stocks traded on the NYSE.

Standard and Poor's 400—measures medium-size companies.

Standard and Poor's 600—measures small-company performance.

New York Stock Exchange Composite—largest composite, tracks all stocks on the NYSE.

American Stock Exchange Market Value Index—tracks roughly 800 companies on the American Exchange.

NASDAQ Composite Index—the NASDAQ consists of many (over 5,500) smaller, lesser-known companies.

Russell 2000—subtracts the 1,000 largest stocks from the top 3,000 to follow smaller capitalization companies. Many small-cap mutual funds compare their returns to this index.

Wilshire 5000—a broad market indicator based on stock of all U.S. companies.

SCULLY STEPS TO SUCCESSFUL INVESTING

Let's review a few guidelines concerning investing in mutual funds or individual stocks:

- ◆ Invest for the long term in assets where your principal can grow.

- ◆ Start out with mutual funds that will give you diversification in many stocks and a money manager who is making investment decisions.

- ◆ Choose funds or individual stocks that represent businesses you are familiar with and you believe in.

- ◆ Look for well-established, well-managed companies with products or services you feel are needed and will be needed in the future.

- ◆ Don't jump on the bandwagon of the most popular stocks (which are usually over-priced)—rather, look for a good value (a relatively low price-to-earnings ratio in a quality stock).

- ◆ Hold for the long term.

- ◆ Don't invest money you will need in the near future.

- ◆ Once you find a company you believe in, buy it and hold it, and you will save a lot of money in commissions.

- ◆ Don't be married to your stock. If you no longer believe in the stock, sell out and move on.

- ◆ Buy low—sell high. Know that the market will fluctuate but, for the long-term, the overall performance of the stock market is headed up. Don't sell when the market goes down or buy when a stock is overpriced.

- ◆ Buy through discount brokers whenever possible. Consider joining or starting an investment club. If you want an advisor, for convenience, timesaving, and professional management, look for a reputable Certified Financial Planner in your area.

- ◆ You can buy your own stocks with just a little research, especially in areas of your expertise.

- ◆ Dollar-cost average, or invest a set amount at regular intervals.

OTHER INVESTMENTS

BONDS AND BOND FUNDS are interest-bearing accounts which do not have the growth potential of stocks. For diversification, many conservative investors will include a percentage of their assets in bonds, especially when approaching retirement.

COLLECTIBLES are a good investment only if you are very knowledgeable and very interested.

SPECULATIVE STOCKS, PENNY STOCKS, COMMODITIES, LOTTERIES, or LAS VEGAS are gambles. Who needs to take this kind of risk when you can achieve your goals easily without it? If you want to gamble, allocate a small amount from your entertainment expense and expect to give this money away.

RECORDING INFORMATION ABOUT YOUR SECURITIES

1. On the annual summary sheet, record annually all securities you currently own, number of shares, date of purchase, cost per share, and total cost.

2. As you make trades during the year and receive statements, record any new transactions on the transaction sheets. Update your portfolio summary at least annually and insert the latest holdings in your binder.

3. Place any trade confirmations in the "Brokerage Transactions" file. File your monthly brokerage statements.

4. I recommend investing in a software program like Quicken or Microsoft Money whenever you begin keeping information about stocks. You can record transactions, update your portfolio automatically from the Internet, and keep your most recent printout in the binder.

Summary of Investment Accounts

Company	Account Name	Account Number	Phone Number	Fax Number

For your personal use, a copy of this form can be found in the back of this book.

Portfolio Summary Stocks/Bonds/Mutual Funds

Year _____

Account Name _____ Account Number _____

Company Name _____ Phone/Fax _____

Stocks/Bonds/Funds	Symbol	Buy Date	#/Share	$/Share	$ Cost
Merck (Example)	MRK	12/1/99	100	92	9200

Transactions for Year _____
Stocks/Bonds/Mutual Funds

Account Name _____ Account Number _____

Company Name _____ Phone/Fax _____

Date	Buy/Sell	Company	#/Share	$/Share	Total	Profit/Loss
1/1/99	Sell	Merck	100	95	9500	$300

For your personal use, a copy of this form can be found in the back of this book.

TAXES
Maximize Your Deductions

Tax returns can be intimidating, but if you break the form down into sections, it's really pretty straightforward.

Report your income: wages, interest, dividends, bonuses, rents, pensions, etc.

Claim deductions: moving expenses, standard deduction or itemized deductions including charitable contributions, interest and taxes paid on business, personal property or mortgages, business expenses, medical expenses, casualty or theft losses, job and miscellaneous expenses, business travel and entertainment, and personal exemptions. Be sure you have supporting documentation for any deductions you take.

Compute your tax: use tables or schedules.

Deduct tax credits: child-care expense, earned income credit, adoption credit.

Deduct taxes withheld and estimated tax payments.

Apply for a refund or send in additional payment due.

Reviewing your tax returns from the previous three years can provide a valuable perspective of your financial situation.

In this section of your binder:

1. Keep copies of the two sides of your 1040 tax returns and comparable state forms for the past three years, which show all the pertinent information you need. The other forms in your tax return just support this summary.

2. Use the tax information sheet to compare your income and taxes from year to year.

3. How much were you able to reduce your taxable income through adjustments and deductions? Here you will see how home interest and taxes, charitable contributions, and other deductions decrease your taxable income.

4. Were you eligible for any tax credits?

5. What was your total federal and state tax? With payroll deductions we don't always realize how much we give to the government.

6. By dividing our total taxes paid by our total income, we see just what percentage of our income went to taxes. Be aware of your changing tax brackets so you are prepared for additional taxes.

7. Your advisors can suggest ways to reduce your taxes. But remember that your investment decisions should be based primarily on what will increase your net worth rather than what will reduce your taxes.

8. Save receipts for anything pertaining to taxes, including W-2s, charitable donation receipts, 1099s, itemized deductions, and real estate transactions, in the tax information file.

Taxes provide many wonderful benefits to our society, and yet we all get frustrated when we think our contributions are being wasted.

I hope this inspires you to VOTE, or better yet, run for office so you can be involved in the good stewardship of this vast amount of capital.

Tax Information

Year _____ _____ _____ _____

Income

Wages				
Interest				
Dividends				
Capital Gain				
Business Income				
Other				
Other				
Total Income				

Adjustments

IRA				
Student Loans				
Medical Savings				
Moving Expenses				
Adjusted Gross Income				

Deductions

Interest Paid				
Taxes Paid				
Medical				
Charitable				
Other				
Taxable Income				

Credits

Child Care				
Education				
Adoption				
Other				

Other Taxes

Other Taxes				
TOTAL FEDERAL TAX				
TOTAL STATE TAX				
% OF TAX/INCOME				

Tax Information Summary

Year_____

Type of Tax	Date Paid	Check No.	Amount
Auto License	_____	_____	_____
. . . .	_____	_____	_____
. . . .	_____	_____	_____
. . . .	_____	_____	_____
. . . .	_____	_____	_____
Personal Property	_____	_____	_____
. . . .	_____	_____	_____
. . . .	_____	_____	_____
. . . .	_____	_____	_____
Home	_____	_____	_____
. . . .	_____	_____	_____
City	_____	_____	_____
State	_____	_____	_____
Federal	_____	_____	_____
Interest Paid	_____	_____	_____
. . . .	_____	_____	_____
. . . .	_____	_____	_____
. . . .	_____	_____	_____
Child-Care Expenses	_____	_____	_____
Income Tax Prep. Exp. . . .	_____	_____	_____
Accounting	_____	_____	_____
Legal Fees	_____	_____	_____
Safety Deposit Box	_____	_____	_____
Professional Bus. Exp. . . .	_____	_____	_____

ESTATE PLANNING
With Preparation Comes Peace

It seems to be a part of human nature to put off making a will. Maybe we believe that if we don't think about death, it won't happen. Consider the option: Die without a will and all your financial affairs become public record. You pay much higher taxes. The government decides how and to whom to pass on whatever is left. Worst of all, you don't choose who will raise your children.

The choice of guardianship for your children should be the primary reason to bite the bullet, face the fact of the grim reaper, and write your desires down in a simple will.

In your will you'll appoint an executor of your estate (a family member or trusted friend) to ensure your wishes are carried out.

A will enables you to minimize court costs and taxes and to choose who will inherit your assets.

If you do not have a will, prepare one and have it witnessed and notarized. Keep the original in your safety deposit box and give copies to your executor and your attorney. Think of it as a final gift of love to your family to have your affairs in order for them.

Estate Planning

A durable economic power of attorney and a health-care power of attorney enable you to designate who is authorized by you to handle decisions if you are incapacitated. Also draw up a living will, which clarifies your wishes concerning life support. Let your family know your desires, and consider donating organs to help others live.

Take this opportunity to talk with your parents about estate planning—yours and theirs. Share this information with them, get their feedback, and open communication for everyone's benefit.

If assets exceed the amount that can be transferred estate-tax free ($675,000 per person for 2000 phasing in to $1,000,000 in 2006), talk to an attorney about gifting (up to $10,000 per year per person) to move some of the money out of the taxable estate. An attorney can help you or your parents establish a simple living trust to pass on much more of your wealth to your loved ones at the death of the second spouse.

If you were to die suddenly, the information you have in your financial planning binder will be invaluable to your executor. Be sure to fill in the information on the estate-planning pages and have your executor sign a signature card authorizing them access to your safety deposit box.

The Emergency Checklist can be filled out and given to whomever is responsible for your home or children in your abscence.

Check off all items that are in your safety deposit box or a fireproof concealed personal safe. Make sure your executor knows the safe's location.

Finally, make a list of any special bequests of personal items you want given to specific loved ones and friends as a remembrance of you. It will give them great solace.

Emergency Checklist

Name _____

Address _____

_____

_____

E-mail Address _____

Web Address _____

Phone (Home) _____

Phone (Work) _____

Pager/Beeper _____

Fax _____

Contact:

Name	**Phone**	**Address**
_____	_____	_____
_____	_____	_____
_____	_____	_____
_____	_____	_____
_____	_____	_____

Alarm Code _____

Alarm Company Phone No. _____

Fire _____

Police _____

Ambulance _____

Doctors _____

_____

Neighbors/Phone No. _____

Notes _____

_____

_____

To My Executor—Estate Planning Summary

Alarm Code _____ **Key to House** _____

Executor of Estate

Name _____

Address _____

_____

Phone _____

Fax _____ E-mail _____

Location of Original Will & Trust

Name _____

Address _____

_____

Phone _____

Guardian of Minor Children

Name _____

Address _____

_____

Phone _____

Trust Officer or Trustee

Name _____

Address _____

_____

Phone _____

Location of the Scully Files—The Blueprint Book/Financial Records

_____

_____

_____

Social Security Numbers

_____

_____

For your personal use, a copy of this form can be found in the back of this book.

Safety Deposit Box

Bank _____

Address _____

_____

_____

Phone_____

Fax _____ E-mail _____

Location of Keys _____

Authorized Access _____

Contents:

❏ Deeds to all property

❏ Car titles/registration

❏ Insurance policies

❏ Titles to all property

❏ Stock, bond, funds certificates (if not

   with broker)

❏ Veterans and military papers

❏ Social Security cards

❏ Retirement agreements

❏ Birth, marriage, and death certificates

❏ Passports

❏ Appraisals

❏ Property improvement receipts

❏ Loan papers

❏ Mortgage papers

❏ Wills

❏ Living wills

❏ Health care power of attorney

❏ Trust papers

❏ Burial requests

❏ Household inventory

❏ Video of personal property

❏ Special bequests

❏ Deeds to all property

❏ Copies of financial forms

_____

_____

_____

_____

_____

_____

_____

PERSONAL ADVISORS
People You Trust

Selecting your advisors is similar to choosing a mate. (Well, there are some significant differences, but I made my point!)

Find people who share your vision and your values, with whom you can communicate completely, and whom you trust implicitly.

They need to be able to listen to you, and to know you, so they can direct you in achieving your goals.

1. Have at least two banking relationships so you can have at least two bids on any loans you negotiate. When you develop a good working relationship with a bank, they will generally go out of their way for you.

2. An excellent accountant is essential, as they observe all your personal and business activities. Consider interviewing a number of accountants to determine their philosophy, fees, and personalities. A good match can last a lifetime.

3. Your accountant (or perhaps acquaintances at church or a friend) can suggest an attorney who can communicate the complexities of law to you in everyday language. It is important to have your own personal attorney to advise you legally on any contracts you sign, to read and explain the fine print, and look out for your interests. If your affairs are complicated, look for a firm that has specialists in real estate, business law, and estate planning.

4. For financial advice, interview the fee-only Certified Financial Planners in your area. Fee-only planners do not take commissions on what they recommend to you, so they are more likely to suggest investments that are in your best interest, and their success is usually tied to your success. Call 888-FEE-ONLY for a list of fee-only advisors in your state. If you have a good relationship with a broker or planner who is paid on commission, just be aware of how much of your potential profit is going to fees and commissions.

Remember there are plenty of advisors with excellent knowledge, and that is essential. But most importantly, you need to be able to communicate with your advisors and understand and respect their judgement, especially when you need them in times of difficulty.

Personal Records

Financial Planner

Name _____

Address _____

_____

Phone _____

Fax _____

Accountant

Name _____

Address _____

_____

Phone _____

Fax _____

Banker

Name _____

Address _____

_____

Phone _____

Fax _____

Banker

Name _____

Address _____

_____

Phone _____

Fax _____

Attorney—Personal

Name _____

Address _____

_____

Phone _____

Fax _____

Attorney—Estate

Name _____

Address _____

_____

Phone _____

Fax _____

Insurance Agent

Name _____

Address _____

_____

Phone _____

Fax _____

Retirement Plan Administrator

Name _____

Address _____

_____

Phone _____

Fax _____

*On the following pages are
duplicates of the forms provided throughout this book.*

Fill free to copy these forms for your personal use.

Her Responses

This is what I heard about money when I was growing up... _____

_____

_____

_____

_____

It made me feel... _____

_____

_____

_____

_____

My greatest fear concerning money is... _____

_____

_____

_____

My greatest hope for our financial future is... _____

_____

_____

_____

My greatest strength when it comes to handling finances is... _____

_____

_____

_____

My greatest weakness in money management is... _____

_____

_____

_____

The one thing I most want to share with you concerning our money is... _____

_____

_____

_____

His Responses

This is what I heard about money when I was growing up... _____
_____
_____
_____
_____

It made me feel... _____
_____
_____
_____
_____

My greatest fear concerning money is... _____
_____
_____
_____

My greatest hope for our financial future is... _____
_____
_____
_____

My greatest strength when it comes to handling finances is... _____
_____
_____
_____

My greatest weakness in money management is... _____
_____
_____
_____

The one thing I most want to share with you concerning our money is... _____
_____
_____
_____

Her Goals

*Date*_____

	1 Year	5 Years	Retirement
1. SPIRITUAL			
2. FAMILY			
3. HEALTH			
4. PROFESSIONAL			
5. COMMUNITY			
6. FINANCIAL			
7. MAJOR PURCHASES			
8. VACATIONS			
9. SOCIAL			
10. HOBBIES & AVOCATIONS			
11. DREAMS			
12. OTHER			

His Goals

*Date*_____

	1 Year	5 Years	Retirement
1. SPIRITUAL			
2. FAMILY			
3. HEALTH			
4. PROFESSIONAL			
5. COMMUNITY			
6. FINANCIAL			
7. MAJOR PURCHASES			
8. VACATIONS			
9. SOCIAL			
10. HOBBIES & AVOCATIONS			
11. DREAMS			
12. OTHER			

Our Goals

Date_____

	1 Year	5 Years	Retirement
1. SPIRITUAL			
2. FAMILY			
3. HEALTH			
4. PROFESSIONAL			
5. COMMUNITY			
6. FINANCIAL			
7. MAJOR PURCHASES			
8. VACATIONS			
9. SOCIAL			
10. HOBBIES & AVOCATIONS			
11. DREAMS			
12. OTHER			

Annual Net Worth Statement

*Date*_____

ASSETS

Current Assets

CASH/CHECKING . . . . _____

CASH/CHECKING 2 . . . . . . _____

SAVINGS . . . . _____

STOCKS . . . . _____

BONDS . . . . _____

MUTUAL FUNDS . . . . _____

OTHER . . . . _____

OTHER . . . . _____

OTHER . . . . _____

TOTAL CURRENT ASSETS

Long-Term Investment Assets

IRA . . . . _____

IRA . . . . _____

OTHER RETIREMENT . . . . . _____

OTHER . . . . _____

OTHER . . . . _____

Personal Use Assets

AUTOMOBILES . . . . _____

PERSONAL PROPERTY . . . . _____

HOME . . . . _____

REAL ESTATE . . . . _____

OTHER . . . . _____

OTHER . . . . _____

OTHER . . . . _____

TOTAL LONG-TERM ASSETS . . . . . . _____

TOTAL ASSETS . . . . _____

LIABILITIES

CREDIT CARD BALANCE . . . _____

_____

_____

Loans:

	Balance	Interest Rate	Annual Payment
HOME	_____	_____	_____
AUTOMOBILES	_____	_____	_____
OTHER	_____	_____	_____
OTHER	_____	_____	_____

TOTAL LIABILITIES . . . . _____

NET WORTH . . . . _____

TOTAL LIABILITIES AND NET WORTH . . . . _____

Net Worth History

YEAR	TOTAL ASSETS	− TOTAL LIABILITIES	= NET WORTH
2000	_____	_____	_____
2001	_____	_____	_____
2002	_____	_____	_____
2003	_____	_____	_____
2004	_____	_____	_____
2005	_____	_____	_____
2006	_____	_____	_____
2007	_____	_____	_____
2008	_____	_____	_____
2009	_____	_____	_____
2010	_____	_____	_____
2011	_____	_____	_____
2012	_____	_____	_____

Monthly Account Balances

Accounts	JAN	FEB	MAR	APR	MAY	JUN	JUL	AUG	SEP	OCT	NOV	DEC

Annual Income/Expenses

	Last Year	This Year's Plan	Monthly Divide Column 2 By 12
INCOME			
SALARY (*Husband*)			
SALARY (*Wife*)			
OTHER			
OTHER			
OTHER			
TOTAL INCOME			
OUTGO			
GOD (*CHARITY*)			
CAESAR (*TAXES*)			
MY DREAMS (*SAVINGS*)			
MY FUTURE (*RETIREMENT*) . .			
NET INCOME			
LIVING EXPENSES			
HOUSING			
HOUSEHOLD/REPAIRS			
FOOD			
CLOTHING			
HEALTH			
EDUCATION			
UTILITIES			
INSURANCE			
TRANSPORTATION			
LOANS			
ENTERTAINMENT/GIFTS			
ACTIVITIES			
CASH/MISCELLANEOUS			
OTHER			
OTHER			
OTHER			
OTHER			
TOTAL OUTGO			
NET			

Monthly Income/Expenses

Year _____

	JAN	FEB	MAR	APR	MAY	JUNE	JULY	AUG	SEPT	OCT	NOV	DEC
INCOME												
SALARY (H)												
SALARY (W)												
OTHER												
OTHER												
OTHER												
TOTAL INCOME												
OUTGO												
GOD (CHARITY)												
CAESAR (TAXES)												
MY DREAMS (SAVINGS)												
MY FUTURE (RETIREMENT)												
NET INCOME												
LIVING EXPENSES												
HOUSING												
HOUSEHOLD/REPAIRS												
FOOD												
CLOTHING												
HEALTH												
EDUCATION												
UTILITIES												
INSURANCE												
TRANSPORTATION												
LOANS												
ENTERTAINMENT/GIFTS												
ACTIVITIES												
CASH/MISCELLANEOUS												
OTHER												
OTHER												
OTHER												
OTHER												
TOTAL OUTGO												
NET												

Charitable Giving

Year _____

Date	Check Number	Charity	Amount
_____	_____	_____	_____
_____	_____	_____	_____
_____	_____	_____	_____
_____	_____	_____	_____
_____	_____	_____	_____
_____	_____	_____	_____
_____	_____	_____	_____
_____	_____	_____	_____
_____	_____	_____	_____
_____	_____	_____	_____
_____	_____	_____	_____
_____	_____	_____	_____
_____	_____	_____	_____
_____	_____	_____	_____
_____	_____	_____	_____
_____	_____	_____	_____
_____	_____	_____	_____
_____	_____	_____	_____
_____	_____	_____	_____
_____	_____	_____	_____
_____	_____	_____	_____
_____	_____	_____	_____
_____	_____	_____	_____
_____	_____	_____	_____
_____	_____	_____	_____
_____	_____	_____	_____

Education

School _____

Address _____

_____

_____

_____

Phone/Fax _____

Tuition _____

_____

Years Attended _____

_____

_____

Degree _____

_____

School _____

Address _____

_____

_____

_____

Phone/Fax _____

Tuition _____

_____

Years Attended _____

_____

_____

Degree _____

_____

School _____

Address _____

_____

_____

_____

Phone/Fax _____

Tuition _____

_____

Years Attended _____

_____

_____

Degree _____

_____

School _____

Address _____

_____

_____

_____

Phone/Fax _____

Tuition _____

_____

Years Attended _____

_____

_____

Degree _____

_____

School _____

Address _____

_____

_____

_____

Phone/Fax _____

Tuition _____

_____

Years Attended _____

_____

_____

Degree _____

_____

School _____

Address _____

_____

_____

_____

Phone/Fax _____

Tuition _____

_____

Years Attended _____

_____

_____

Degree _____

_____

Job History/Resumé

Job History

Company _____
Years _____
Address _____
_____
_____
_____

Phone _____
Reference _____
_____
_____

Company _____
Years _____
Address _____
_____
_____

Phone _____
Reference _____
_____
_____

Company _____
Years _____
Address _____
_____
_____

Phone _____
Reference _____
_____
_____

Company _____
Years _____
Address _____
_____
_____

Phone _____
Reference _____
_____

Professional Societies & Organizations

_____
_____
_____
_____
_____
_____
_____
_____
_____
_____
_____
_____
_____
_____

Research & Publications

_____
_____
_____
_____
_____
_____
_____
_____

Awards & Honors

_____
_____
_____
_____
_____
_____
_____
_____

Family Medical Information

Family Information

Name _____

Address _____

_____

_____

Phone_____

Phone (Work) _____

Fax _____

Soc. Sec. No. _____

Date of Birth _____

Place of Birth_____

Passport No. _____

Notes _____

_____

Immunizations & Medical Notes

Physician _____

Address _____

_____

Phone_____

Fax _____

Dentist _____

Address _____

_____

Phone_____

Fax _____

Name _____

Address _____

_____

_____

Phone _____

Phone (Work) _____

Fax _____

Soc. Sec. No. _____

Date of Birth _____

Place of Birth_____

Passport No. _____

Notes _____

_____

Physician _____

Address _____

_____

Phone_____

Fax _____

Dentist _____

Address _____

_____

Phone_____

Fax _____

Name _____

Address _____

_____

_____

Phone _____

Phone (Work) _____

Fax _____

Soc. Sec. No. _____

Date of Birth _____

Place of Birth_____

Passport No. _____

Notes _____

_____

Physician _____

Address _____

_____

Phone_____

Fax _____

Dentist _____

Address _____

_____

Phone_____

Fax _____

Medical/Dental Payments

Name of Family Member and Doctor	Date of Visit	Amount of Charge	Amount Ins. Paid	Deductable Satified? YES	NO	Co-Pay Amt. Paid	$ Paid out of Pocket
_____ _____	_____	_____	_____	❑	❑	_____	_____
_____ _____	_____	_____	_____	❑	❑	_____	_____
_____ _____	_____	_____	_____	❑	❑	_____	_____
_____ _____	_____	_____	_____	❑	❑	_____	_____
_____ _____	_____	_____	_____	❑	❑	_____	_____
_____ _____	_____	_____	_____	❑	❑	_____	_____
_____ _____	_____	_____	_____	❑	❑	_____	_____
_____ _____	_____	_____	_____	❑	❑	_____	_____
_____ _____	_____	_____	_____	❑	❑	_____	_____
_____ _____	_____	_____	_____	❑	❑	_____	_____

Bank Accounts

Name of Bank _____

Address _____

_____

Bank's Web Address _____

Banker _____

Banker's E-mail _____

Phone _____

Fax _____

Account No. _____

_____

_____

_____

Access/ATM Card No. _____

Notes: _____

_____

_____

_____

_____

_____

_____

_____

_____

_____

_____

_____

_____

Name of Bank _____

Address _____

_____

Bank's Web Address _____

Banker _____

Banker's E-mail _____

Phone _____

Fax _____

Account No. _____

_____

_____

_____

Access/ATM Card No. _____

Notes: _____

_____

_____

_____

_____

_____

_____

_____

_____

_____

_____

_____

_____

Name of Bank _____

Address _____

_____

Bank's Web Address _____

Banker _____

Banker's E-mail _____

Phone _____

Fax _____

Account No. _____

_____

_____

_____

Access/ATM Card No. _____

Notes: _____

_____

_____

_____

_____

_____

_____

_____

_____

_____

_____

_____

_____

Car Information

Make and Model _____

Year _____

Purchase Date _____

Odometer Reading _____

Purchase Cost _____

Sales Tax _____

Title No. _____

ID No. _____

Purchased From _____

Address _____

_____

_____

_____

Service Record

Who Performs Service _____

Service Phone No. _____

Major Repairs _____

_____

_____

_____

_____

_____

Contact _____

Phone No. _____

E-mail _____

Make and Model _____

Year _____

Purchase Date _____

Odometer Reading _____

Purchase Cost _____

Sales Tax _____

Title No. _____

ID No. _____

Purchased From _____

Address _____

_____

_____

_____

Service Record

Who Performs Service _____

Service Phone No. _____

Major Repairs _____

_____

_____

_____

_____

_____

Contact _____

Phone No. _____

E-mail _____

Make and Model _____

Year _____

Purchase Date _____

Odometer Reading _____

Purchase Cost _____

Sales Tax _____

Title No. _____

ID No. _____

Purchased From _____

Address _____

_____

_____

_____

Service Record

Who Performs Service _____

Service Phone No. _____

Major Repairs _____

_____

_____

_____

_____

_____

Contact _____

Phone No. _____

E-mail _____

Real Estate Information

Date of Purchase _____   Address _____

Purchase Price _____   _____

Date of Sale _____   _____

Selling Price _____   _____

Home Information

Date   **Improvement**   **Cost**

_____

_____

_____

_____

_____

_____

_____

_____

_____

_____

_____

_____

_____

_____

_____

_____

_____

_____

_____

_____

_____

_____

_____

_____

_____

_____

_____

_____

Keep a copy of your closing statement and receipts from all major purchases and improvements, which add to the value of your home.

Home Inventory

Major purchases	Date	Cost	Serial #	Warranty

Other: _____

Insurance

Automobile

Company _____ Policy # _____

Address _____ Agent _____

_____ Phone # _____

Coverage _____

_____ Cost _____

Homeowners

Company _____ Policy # _____

Address _____ Agent _____

_____ Phone # _____

Coverage _____

_____ Cost _____

Medical

Company _____ Policy # _____

Address _____ Agent _____

_____ Phone # _____

Coverage _____

_____ Cost _____

Life

Company _____ Policy # _____

Address _____ Agent _____

_____ Phone # _____

Coverage _____

_____ Cost _____

Disability

Company _____ Policy # _____

Address _____ Agent _____

_____ Phone # _____

Coverage _____

_____ Cost _____

Liability

Company _____ Policy # _____

Address _____ Agent _____

_____ Phone # _____

Coverage _____

_____ Cost _____

Other Insurance

Type of Insurance _____

Company _____ Policy # _____

Address _____ Agent _____

_____ Phone # _____

Coverage _____

_____ Cost _____

Type of Insurance _____

Company _____ Policy # _____

Address _____ Agent _____

_____ Phone # _____

Coverage _____

_____ Cost _____

Type of Insurance _____

Company _____ Policy # _____

Address _____ Agent _____

_____ Phone # _____

Coverage _____

_____ Cost _____

Type of Insurance _____

Company _____ Policy # _____

Address _____ Agent _____

_____ Phone # _____

Coverage _____

_____ Cost _____

Type of Insurance _____

Company _____ Policy # _____

Address _____ Agent _____

_____ Phone # _____

Coverage _____

_____ Cost _____

Type of Insurance _____

Company _____ Policy # _____

Address _____ Agent _____

_____ Phone # _____

Coverage _____

_____ Cost _____

Retirement

Name of Account _____

Policy # _____

Phone _____

Fax_____

E-mail _____

Agent _____

Company_____

Address_____

Date _____

Beneficiary _____

Terms — vesting schedule _____

_____

_____

Name of Account _____

Policy # _____

Phone _____

Fax_____

E-mail _____

Agent _____

Company_____

Address_____

Date _____

Beneficiary _____

Terms — vesting schedule _____

_____

_____

Name of Account _____

Policy # _____

Phone _____

Fax_____

E-mail _____

Agent _____

Company _____

Address_____

Date _____

Beneficiary _____

Terms — vesting schedule _____

_____

_____

Credit Cards

Credit Card Company _____   **Notes:** _____
Account No. _____   _____
Phone_____   _____
Name on Card _____   _____
Interest Rate _____   _____

Credit Card Company _____   **Notes:** _____
Account No. _____   _____
Phone_____   _____
Name on Card _____   _____
Interest Rate _____   _____

Credit Card Company _____   **Notes:** _____
Account No. _____   _____
Phone_____   _____
Name on Card _____   _____
Interest Rate _____   _____

Credit Card Company _____   **Notes:** _____
Account No. _____   _____
Phone_____   _____
Name on Card _____   _____
Interest Rate _____   _____

Credit Card Company _____   **Notes:** _____
Account No. _____   _____
Phone_____   _____
Name on Card _____   _____
Interest Rate _____   _____

Credit Card Company _____   **Notes:** _____
Account No. _____   _____
Phone_____   _____
Name on Card _____   _____
Interest Rate _____   _____

Credit Card Company _____   **Notes:** _____
Account No. _____   _____
Phone_____   _____
Name on Card _____   _____
Interest Rate _____   _____

Loans

Original Loan Amount _____

Date	Interest Rate	Balance	Payment

Home Mortgage _____

Bank _____

Contact _____ Notes _____

Address _____ _____

_____ _____

E-mail _____ _____

Phone/Fax _____ _____

Loan # _____ _____

Original Loan Amount _____

Date	Interest Rate	Balance	Payment

Second Mortgage _____

Bank _____

Contact _____ Notes _____

Address _____ _____

_____ _____

E-mail _____ _____

Phone/Fax _____ _____

Loan # _____ _____

Original Loan Amount _____

Date	Interest Rate	Balance	Payment

Automobile _____

Bank _____

Contact _____ Notes _____

Address _____ _____

_____ _____

E-mail _____ _____

Phone/Fax _____ _____

Loan # _____ _____

Original Loan Amount _____

Date	Interest Rate	Balance	Payment

Second Automobile _____

Bank _____

Contact _____ Notes _____

Address _____ _____

_____ _____

E-mail _____ _____

Phone/Fax _____ _____

Loan # _____ _____

Loans

Original Balance _____

Date	Interest Rate	Balance	Payment

Other Loans _____

Bank _____

Contact _____

Address _____

_____

E-mail _____

Phone/Fax _____

Loan # _____

Notes _____

_____

_____

_____

_____

_____

Original Balance _____

Date	Interest Rate	Balance	Payment

Other Loans _____

Bank _____

Contact _____

Address _____

_____

E-mail _____

Phone/Fax _____

Loan # _____

Notes _____

_____

_____

_____

_____

_____

Original Balance _____

Date	Interest Rate	Balance	Payment

Other Loans _____

Bank _____

Contact _____

Address _____

_____

E-mail _____

Phone/Fax _____

Loan # _____

Notes _____

_____

_____

_____

_____

_____

Original Balance _____

Date	Interest Rate	Balance	Payment

Other Loans _____

Bank _____

Contact _____

Address _____

_____

E-mail _____

Phone/Fax _____

Loan # _____

Notes _____

_____

_____

_____

_____

_____

Summary of Investment Accounts

Company	Account Name	Account Number	Phone Number	Fax Number

Portfolio Summary Stocks/Bonds/Mutual Funds

Year_____

Account Name _____ Account Number _____

Company Name _____ Phone/Fax _____

Stocks/Bonds/Funds	Symbol	Buy Date	#/Share	$/Share	$ Cost
Merck (Example)	MRK	12/1/99	100	92	9200

Transactions for Year _____
Stocks/Bonds/Mutual Funds

Account Name _____ Account Number _____

Company Name _____ Phone/Fax _____

Date	Buy/Sell	Company	#/Share	$/Share	Total	Profit/Loss
1/1/99	Sell	Merck	100	95	9500	$300

Tax Information

Year _____ _____ _____ _____

Income

Wages				
Interest				
Dividends				
Capital Gain				
Business Income				
Other				
Other				
Total Income				

Adjustments

IRA				
Student Loans				
Medical Savings				
Moving Expenses				
Adjusted Gross Income				

Deductions

Interest Paid				
Taxes Paid				
Medical				
Charitable				
Other				
Taxable Income				

Credits

Child Care				
Education				
Adoption				
Other				

Other Taxes

TOTAL FEDERAL TAX				
TOTAL STATE TAX				
% OF TAX/INCOME				

Tax Information Summary

Year_____

Type of Tax	Date Paid	Check No.	Amount
Auto License			
. . . .			
. . . .			
. . . .			
. . . .			
Personal Property			
. . . .			
. . . .			
. . . .			
Home			
. . . .			
City			
State			
Federal			
Interest Paid			
. . . .			
. . . .			
. . . .			
Child-Care Expenses			
Income Tax Prep. Exp. . . .			
Accounting			
Legal Fees			
Safety Deposit Box			
Professional Bus. Exp. . . .			

Emergency Checklist

Name _____

Address _____

_____

_____

E-mail Address _____

Web Address _____

Phone (Home) _____

Phone (Work) _____

Pager/Beeper _____

Fax _____

Contact:

Name	Phone	Address

Alarm Code _____

Alarm Company Phone No. _____

Fire _____

Police _____

Ambulance _____

Doctors _____

_____

Neighbors/Phone No. _____

Notes _____

_____

_____

To My Executor—Estate Planning Summary

Alarm Code _____ **Key to House** _____

Executor of Estate

Name _____

Address _____

_____

Phone _____

Fax _____ E-mail _____

Location of Original Will & Trust

Name _____

Address _____

_____

Phone _____

Guardian of Minor Children

Name _____

Address _____

_____

Phone _____

Trust Officer or Trustee

Name _____

Address _____

_____

Phone _____

Location of the Scully Files—The Blueprint Book/Financial Records

_____

_____

_____

Social Security Numbers

_____

_____

Safety Deposit Box

Bank _____

Address _____

_____

_____

Phone_____

Fax _____ E-mail _____

Location of Keys _____

Authorized Access _____

Contents:

❑ Deeds to all property

❑ Car titles/registration

❑ Insurance policies

❑ Titles to all property

❑ Stock, bond, funds certificates (if not

    with broker)

❑ Veterans and military papers

❑ Social Security cards

❑ Retirement agreements

❑ Birth, marriage, and death certificates

❑ Passports

❑ Appraisals

❑ Property improvement receipts

❑ Loan papers

❑ Mortgage papers

❑ Wills

❑ Living wills

❑ Health care power of attorney

❑ Trust papers

❑ Burial requests

❑ Household inventory

❑ Video of personal property

❑ Special bequests

❑ Deeds to all property

❑ Copies of financial forms

_____

_____

_____

_____

_____

_____

_____

Personal Advisors

Financial Planner

Name _____

Address _____

_____

Phone _____

Fax _____

Accountant

Name _____

Address _____

_____

Phone _____

Fax _____

Banker

Name _____

Address _____

_____

Phone _____

Fax _____

Banker

Name _____

Address _____

_____

Phone _____

Fax _____

Attorney—Personal

Name _____

Address _____

_____

Phone _____

Fax _____

Attorney—Estate

Name _____

Address _____

_____

Phone _____

Fax _____

Insurance Agent

Name _____

Address _____

_____

Phone _____

Fax _____

Retirement Plan Administrator

Name _____

Address _____

_____

Phone _____

Fax _____

References

The purpose of **The Scully Files** is to start as many couples as possible on the right path toward financial intimacy and independence. I have included a list of references that I have found informative, insightful, and personally inspirational. I hope they are helpful to you as you continue on your journey.

Books

The Bible

God Calling, by A.J. Russell (Editor). Barbour & Co.

*The Holy Use of Money: Personal Finance in Light of Christian Faith, by John C. Haughey, S.J. Doubleday & Company

The Richest Man in Babylon, by George S. Clason. New American Library.

The 7 Habits of Highly Effective People, by Stephen R. Covey. Fireside.

The 9 Steps to Financial Freedom, by Suze Orman. Crown Publishing.

The Intelligent Investor: A Book of Practical Counsel, by Benjamin Graham. HarperCollins.

*The Money Book of Personal Finance, by Richard Eisenberg. Warner Books.

Kiplinger's Practical Guide to Investing, by Ted Miller. Kiplinger Books.

Your Money or Your Life, by Joe Dominguez and Vicki Robin. Penguin USA.

Stocks for the Long Run: The Definitive Guide to Financial Market Returns and Long-Term Investment Strategies, by Jeremy Siegel. McGraw-Hill.

How to Make Money in Stocks: A Winning System in Good Times and Bad, by William J. O'Neil. McGraw-Hill.

The Wall Street Journal Guide to Understanding Money and Investing, by Kenneth M. Morris, et al. Fireside.

The Roaring 2000s: Building the Wealth and Lifestyle You Desire in the Greatest Boom in History, by Harry S. Dent, Jr. Touchstone Books.

One Up on Wall Street: How to Use What You Already Know to Make Money in the Market, by Peter Lynch and John Rothchild. Penguin USA.

Financial Peace, by Dave Ramsey and Sharon Ramsey. Viking Press.

Soulmates: Honoring the Mysteries of Love and Relationship, by Thomas Moore. Harper Collins.

*out of print—check your library

Network and Cable Television Financial Programs

Nightly Business Report, PBS

Wall Street Week, PBS

CNBC/FNN

Periodicals

Money Magazine

Smart Money

Individual Investor

Business Week

Forbes

Newspapers

Wall Street Journal

USA Today

Investor's Business Daily

Barron's National Business & Financial Weekly

Newsletters

BottomLine

Kiplinger's Washington Letter

Personal Finance

Research Reports

Value Line Investment Survey (Stock analysis)

Standard & Poor's (Stocks, Bonds, Insurance)

Mergent FIS (formerly Moody's Investor Service)(Insurance Companies)

Morningstar (Mutual fund analysis)

A.M. Best Company (Insurance Company Rating Service)

Web Sites

www.bankrate.com (Interest Rate Information from Credit Cards to Home Mortgage)

www.hsh.com (Mortgage Information)

www.investorsguide.com

www.smartmoney.com

www.ms.com

Author's Biography

Bonnie Baron Scully grew up in an Air Force family, living in Alaska, Ohio, New Mexico, Alabama, Florida, California, Virginia, South Dakota, Iowa, and North Carolina. She has traveled extensively throughout the world.

She graduated from Spring Hill College in Mobile, Alabama with a bachelor's degree in English and a minor in Psychology, and received her teaching credentials through Virginia Commonwealth University. A graduate of the College for Financial Planning in Denver, she attained her Certified Financial Planner designation in 1986. She is a member of the Financial Planning Association and the Institute of Certified Financial Planners.

Currently she is actively involved in financial counseling through her books, seminars and involvement with Engaged Encounter. Her previous book is *The Scully Files, Organizing Your Finances—A Spiritually Oriented Guide to Managing Your Money*.

Bonnie's career has been quite diverse. She has worked as a Certified Financial Planner with Parsec Financial Management, as a business and financial advisor, and as the Chairman of the Airline and Travel Career Program at the National College of Business. Ealier in her career, she worked as an elementary school teacher, tax preparer, travel agent, and as a flight attendant for Delta Airlines.

Bonnie has been married for 29 years to her college sweetheart, Bob, who is an oral and maxillofacial surgeon in Asheville, North Carolina. They have been blessed with two children.

Since she and her husband settled in Western North Carolina in 1980, Bonnie has been very active in the community. She has participated in Leadership Asheville, United Way, Hospice, and the Parish Council for St. Joan of Arc Church. She has worked on the boards of Junior Achievement, Children's Home Society, the Jesuit House of Prayer, and the Foundation of the Roman Catholic Diocese of Charlotte. She has served as president of the school board and the Parent-Faculty Association at Asheville Catholic School, and president of the Buncombe County Dental Auxiliary. She has also been active on the Bele Chere Entertainment Committee and the St. Joseph's Hospital Special Events Committee. She is listed in Marquis Who's Who in America, Marquis Who's Who in Business and Finance and Who's Who of American Women, Millenium Edition.

Her personal interests include writing, yoga, traveling, and spending time with her family.

My Wish for You as You Begin Your Journey

I hope and pray that this book will provide you with insights that will empower your relationship and bring you peace when it comes to managing your money. Finances are just one of the many exciting parts of the journey that we share as loving couples. May your shared experiences bring you joy, thanksgiving, and opportunities to express the spirit of love. Good luck, God bless you, and remember, in all your decisions—only what is done with love will last! I leave you with the lyrics to a beautiful song, and my wish for you of a lifetime of "love so strong".

— Bonnie Baron Scully

Love So Strong

By Joe Mattingly

By your side I stand, turn and take your hand.
Praise the Lord above who has blessed this love.
In your eyes I see all that God's revealed,
We are young and love is very strong.
Side by side we stand, here as one.
And throughout the years, with their joys and tears,
As the storms pass through, I will shelter you.
When our music plays, we shall dance all day.
We shall laugh and cry, we shall sing.
When the music plays, we shall sing.
And our children's love, gift from God above.
Take their hands each day, help them learn to pray.
And when in our arms, feel those hearts beat on.
All our love reflected in their eyes—in their eyes.
And as we grow old, will that fire turn cold?
Will we say we love, as we love today?
Will our eyes still meet, or will passion cease?
Will the years be all that we feel? Will the years be all we feel?
By your side I wake, feel your warmth, touch your face.
Yes I love you more than I did at first.
Feel the magic of, of our first sweet kiss.
We are old and our love's very strong.
All throughout the years, still as strong.
Love so strong.

*I appreciate the authorizations for: the lyrics of **Love So Strong** by Joe Mattingly, Copyright 1995, World Library Publications. 800-621-5197. Schiller Park, Il 60176. All rights reserved. Used by permission: the opening quote from **The Angel of Bengal, The Life and Teachings of Mother Rytasha** by Razaque Khan, ISBN 984-31-0362.9; and the photogragh on page 7 by S & S Photographers, Huntsville, Alabama.*

Order Forms

Name _____

Address _____

_____

City _____

State _____ Zip _____

Daytime Phone (_____) _____

(In case we need to clarify your order)

Please send orders
and checks payable to:

The Scully Files
SpiritSource Publications
P.O. Box 18074
Asheville, NC 28814

Thank you for your order!

Quantity ordered		Price each	Total Price
	A Young Couple's Blueprint for Managing Money	**$14.95**	
5% discount for 5 to 9 books *10% discount for 10 or more books*	N.C. residents add 6% sales tax $.90 x number of books	.90	
	Shipping and Handling $4.00 for first book. $2.00 for each additional book	4.00	
	Total enclosed		

- -

Name _____

Address _____

_____

City _____

State _____ Zip _____

Daytime Phone (_____) _____

(In case we need to clarify your order)

Please send orders
and checks payable to:

The Scully Files
SpiritSource Publications
P.O. Box 18074
Asheville, NC 28814

Thank you for your order!

Quantity ordered		Price each	Total Price
	A Young Couple's Blueprint for Managing Money	**$14.95**	
5% discount for 5 to 9 books *10% discount for 10 or more books*	N.C. residents add 6% sales tax $.90 x number of books	.90	
	Shipping and Handling $4.00 for first book. $2.00 for each additional book	4.00	
	Total enclosed		

Please visit my web site **www.thescullyfiles.com** for additional ordering options
and more information on **The Scully Files**.

Order Forms

Name _____

Address _____

_____

City _____

State _____ Zip _____

Daytime Phone (_____) _____

(In case we need to clarify your order)

Please send orders
and checks payable to:

The Scully Files
SpiritSource Publications
P.O. Box 18074
Asheville, NC 28814

Thank you for your order!

Quantity ordered		Price each	Total Price
	A Young Couple's Blueprint for Managing Money	$14.95	
5% discount for 5 to 9 books	N.C. residents add 6% sales tax $.90 x number of books	.90	
10% discount for 10 or more books	Shipping and Handling $4.00 for first book. $2.00 for each additional book	4.00	
		Total enclosed	

Name _____

Address _____

_____

City _____

State _____ Zip _____

Daytime Phone (_____) _____

(In case we need to clarify your order)

Please send orders
and checks payable to:

The Scully Files
SpiritSource Publications
P.O. Box 18074
Asheville, NC 28814

Thank you for your order!

Quantity ordered		Price each	Total Price
	A Young Couple's Blueprint for Managing Money	$14.95	
5% discount for 5 to 9 books	N.C. residents add 6% sales tax $.90 x number of books	.90	
10% discount for 10 or more books	Shipping and Handling $4.00 for first book. $2.00 for each additional book	4.00	
		Total enclosed	

Please visit my web site **www.thescullyfiles.com** for additional ordering options
and more information on **The Scully Files**.

Notes

Notes